# INTRODUCTION TO ORTHODOX CANON LAW

## LEWIS J. PATSAVOS

# HOLY CROSS
ORTHODOX PRESS

Brookline, Massachusetts

ISBN: 978-1-960613-00-4

Publisher's Cataloging-in-Publication
(Provided by Cassidy Cataloguing Services, Inc.).
Names:  Patsavos, Ēlias I., author. | Calivas, Alkiviadis C., writer of
        foreword.
Title: Introduction to Orthodox canon law / Lewis J. Patsavos ; foreword
        by Fr. Alkiviadis C. Calivas.
Description: Brookline, MA : Holy Cross Orthodox Press, [2023] |
            Includes bibliographical references.
Identifiers: ISBN: 978-1-960613-00-4 (paperback)
Subjects: LCSH: Canon law--Orthodox Eastern Church. | Nomocanon.
          | Church polity. | Orthodox Eastern Church--Government. |
          Greek Orthodox Archdiocese of North and South America--
          Government.
Classification: LCC: KBS716 .P38 2023 | DDC: 262.9/819--dc23

# TABLE OF CONTENTS

## FOREWORD

In every generation the Holy Spirit inspires certain devout and faithful persons to devote their lives to the study of the mysteries of the Orthodox faith. These people are the theologians of the Church, who by faith and education work diligently to articulate the Church's faith. Theologians labor, not only to defend, but also to interpret the eternal truths revealed by Christ and taught by the Holy Spirit (John 14:25–26; 16:12–15); truths which are deposited in the Church in both Scripture and Tradition.

Over time, the science of theology has developed into several distinct but interrelated fields of study classified under the headings of biblical, historical, dogmatic, patristic, and practical or applied theology. Together these several disciplines—albeit from a different yet complementary perspective—form a whole, since each specialty probes and contemplates the same divine truth revealed by Christ; proclaimed by the prophets, apostles, fathers, and Holy Synods; and taught by the Church, the "pillar and bulwark of the truth" (1 Tim 3:15).

The category of applied or practical theology contains several disciplines, among which are liturgics, pastoral care, homiletics, religious education, the liturgical arts, and canon law, the latter being the subject of the important volume in hand, Introduction to Orthodox Canon Law, authored by the learned, cultured, and devout lay theologian, Dr. Lewis J. Patsavos, a trusted colleague and beloved brother in the Lord.

Doing theology for the Church is a vital ministry. The theologian is called to discern and teach the truths of the faith and to do this in a comprehensive, coherent, and responsible manner, according to his or her God-given abilities. Professor Lewis J. Patsavos has performed this ministry with success and exemplary dedication for more than half a century, the greater part of which was spent as a distinguished member of the faculty of Holy Cross Greek Orthodox School of Theology.

Prior to his appointment to the faculty in 1974, Canon Law at Holy Cross was restricted to a single course, which was taught by individuals from a related field. All that changed. Professor Patsavos enriched the curriculum through his required and elective course offerings in Canon Law. An area hitherto lacking was now enlivened and enhanced. Thanks to his expert understanding of the complex dimensions of the canonical tradition, Professor Patsavos was able to give greater depth to the subject, resulting in the heightened interest of the students and their increased appreciation for the pastoral dimensions of the canons, a characteristic which Dr. Patsavos has labored to make evident in all his writings; particularly in this significant volume, Introduction to Orthodox Canon Law.

In addition to his teaching responsibilities, Professor Patsavos was often asked to provide church officials with a variety of opinions on canonical matters, ecclesial charters, and parish regulations. Through his participation in various pan-Orthodox and ecumenical consultations, hierarchs, clergy, and colleagues came to respect and appreciate his soft-spoken manners and the clear and balanced reflections that are as evident in his writings as in his personal interactions.

Soon after his appointment to the faculty of Holy Cross, Dr. Patsavos was also appointed Director of Field Education, a position he held for several decades. This pairing of disciplines reflects the field of applied theology. As Dr. Patsavos puts it in the pages below: "Canon Law is the discipline that seeks to bridge the gulf between the ideal model of Christian life and the reality of the struggle in which the Church exists." The Field Education Brochure of Holy Cross, which he helped create, notes: "Theological studies cannot be separated or unrelated to church life or be detached from the life of God's people. Field Education seeks to provide the student with a comprehensive and realistic view of the Church and its role in the lives of persons."

Through his scholarly work, Professor Patsavos has labored conscientiously and effectively to help God's people—clergy and laity alike—to understand and appreciate the canonical tradition of the Church. Through his teaching, articles, and written opinions to hierarchs on specific canonical questions Dr. Patsavos has made it clear that the canons are not, as some believe, a set of lifeless regulations but vital agents for the protection and promotion of the orderly life of the Church.

Canon Law may well be the most misunderstood discipline of Orthodox theology. In large measure, the volume in hand, Introduction to Orthodox Canon Law, sets out to correct these misunderstandings and uphold the perennial value of the Church's venerable canonical tradition. It may well be Professor Patsavos' most important scholarly achievement because in this case it fills a specific void—the absence until now of a reasoned and cogent text in the English language with which to navigate the canonical tradition of the Orthodox Church.

Introduction to Orthodox Canon Law is clearly a labor of love, stamped by years of experience and devotion to the theological enterprise. Through his lucid and eloquent linguistic skills, Dr. Lewis Patsavos imparts an appreciation for the essential pastoral nature of the holy canons. The divine truths deposited in the Church are embedded in her liturgical and canonical tradition. The canons, therefore, are not dead rules but an expression of how theological truths are applied in specific historical circumstances. They are meant to help both persons and communities realize the highest excellence. By setting such a standard, the canons uphold the basic truths of the gospel as they apply to personal and communal living.

Fr. Alkiviadis C. Calivas,
Professor of Liturgics, Emeritus
Holy Cross Greek Orthodox School of Theology

## PREFACE

My students sometimes ask me why I chose to specialize in canon law, perhaps the most controversial and misunderstood subject among all the theological disciplines in our curriculum. My response often comes as a surprise: it was *obedience*—a valid canonical principle—to my spiritual father and mentor, Archbishop Iakovos of North and South America. When I sought his counsel about which field of study to pursue, he exhorted: "You must study canon law. We need canonists desperately!" I was stunned, but I obeyed, and I did not regret it.

Another telling experience reminiscent of the way I was led into canon law took place at the beginning of my full-time teaching career at Holy Cross School of Theology in 1974. The need to develop a more adequate practical training experience in ministry had become apparent. Previously, ministerial training had amounted to little more than the random assignment of students to parishes in the hope that they would experience all they needed to know about parish ministry. Improving this system meant introducing a new component into the curriculum—theological field education. Such a goal, however, would require hiring another member of the faculty to oversee this demanding endeavor. At the faculty meeting convened to discuss the matter, there was reluctance to support the proposed solution due to financial considerations. Faced with this difficult situation, the dean looked directly at me—then the newest member of the faculty—and exclaimed: "Dr. Patsavos will be responsible for this new assignment!"

Once again, I was stunned, but submitted to the call with obedience. Once again, I never regretted the decision. On the contrary, the double responsibility of teaching canon law and directing the Field Education Program at Holy Cross enabled me to experience the pastoral nature of the canons contextually through theological field education. I began to see how this new component in our curriculum interfaced ideally with the study of canon law.

What follows, then, is an attempt to show the pastoral dimension of the canons evident in their application by the Church. This is one component that influenced my teaching of canon law. Another is the engagement in ecumenical dialogue facilitated by participating for over twenty-five years in the North American Orthodox–Catholic Bilateral Consultation. It was here that the canonical dimension of many contemporary issues became evident. Issues such as *oikonomia*, ecclesiology, marriage, primacy, and conciliarity, among others, offered ample opportunity for study and reflection, and were a valuable resource for integration into my course material.

The result of these experiences led me to prepare what I have chosen to call an *Introduction to Orthodox Canon Law*. This *Introduction* is the compiled prose version of notes used for the class in Orthodox canon law taught at Holy Cross School of Theology throughout my teaching career. Hence, it is not a textbook or an exhaustive study in Orthodox canon law. It is an offering in response to the request of former students wishing to review what they were taught in the past, and of interested laypersons aspiring to learn something about which they know little. Given this modest request, it does not delve into detail about a subject that is little known and much misunderstood. Rather, it provides a general introduction and foundation. This was in fact the goal of the course in Orthodox canon law. Furthermore, this work is meant to be read and understood primarily by those with a thirst to expand their overall knowledge of the Orthodox faith. As a component of the theological disciplines that compose this faith, it is inconceivable for one seeking to learn and experience the faith not to be conversant with its canonical tradition.

It is expected, therefore, that the reader who absorbs the content of this brief study will seek to expand that knowledge by exploring the canons themselves. Fortified with a basic understanding of the manner in which the canons should be read and interpreted, one may begin to explore a vast new body of rare knowledge.

The eager student will soon find that the challenge confronting the interpreter of the canons is unique. We seek to convey the truth of the written word that guides us in our spiritual journey through life. It is our special task to convey this truth through application to the life of the contemporary Church. Although more literal interpretive methods exist, correct application to the present day can only be achieved by relating the canons to their historical context. This more clearly underscores the spirit of the canons, but attempting it requires a thorough background in the theological disciplines. The challenge of interpretation must be met by identifying the historical circumstances that led to the creation of applicable canons and relating their enduring principles to the needs of the Church today.

The content of this publication reflects the generally held principles of the canonical tradition throughout the Orthodox Church. Where variations may exist in canonical practice, they have been identified. This is especially the case with variations in practice that may apply to Orthodox jurisdictions in America. This is in keeping with the characteristic flexibility of the Orthodox canonical tradition to meet the local needs of the Church. While these practices may be adapted to circumstances, the essence of the faith must remain immutable.

Where I have expanded on particular subjects in various publications written for other purposes, they have been included as an appendix.

It is my fervent hope that the expectations of those who read this *Introduction to Orthodox Canon Law* will be met and that the experience gained thereby will prepare them for a proper understanding of this misunderstood discipline.

I am indebted to numerous persons, especially former students, who urged me to prepare a text based on notes used for the course taught in Orthodox Canon Law. The result is this publication of Introduction to Orthodox Canon Law. Throughout its phases of preparation, I was encouraged by my esteemed friend and colleague, Rev. Dr. Alkiviadis Calivas, whose wise suggestions are greatly appreciated. I am also deeply honored by his willingness to write the foreword.

Others, too, in ways in which they may not have been aware, contributed to the realization of this work in its later stages: His Grace the Rt. Rev. Dr. Joachim Cotsonis for his invaluable assistance in the use of the Holy Cross Library and its resources, the V. Rev. Dr. Fr. Anton Vrame for according numerous courtesies of the press, and President George Cantonis of Hellenic College - Holy Cross for his ongoing encouragement and support of this project. In addition, I wish to gratefully acknowledge the role of those who contributed in a variety of other ways to its materialization: Professor Timothy Patitsas, Sister Nectaria McLees, Rev. Bartholomew Mercado, Ashley Carr, John Carr, Andreas MacLean, William Redmon, Jonathan Resmini, Peter Schadler, and Kyle Sterner.

I am particularly beholden to Rev. Professor Patrick Viscuso for his close collaboration in revising sections of the original text of this work, especially those dealing with marriage, which is his area of specialization.

To all the above I owe a debt of lasting gratitude.

## NOTE ON SOURCE MATERIAL

*Introduction to Orthodox Canon Law* is based on the unpublished lectures of my respected teacher Professor Constantine Mouratides, listed under the heading Κανονικὸν Δίκαιον (Canon Law), as well as on sections from the classic canon law textbook of N. Milaš, Τὸ Ἐκκλησιαστικὸν Δίκαιον τῆς Ἀνατολικῆς Ὀρθοδόξου Ἐκκλησίας (The Ecclesiastical Law of the Eastern Orthodox Church).

Where appropriate, adjustments have been made to conform to canonical practice in the Greek Orthodox Archdiocese of America. Where other secondary sources have been used, they are duly identified. Scriptural texts are from the New King James Version (NKJV) of the Bible. Canonical texts, unless otherwise identified, are from the editor H. Percival's *The Seven Ecumenical Councils* in the series *Nicene and Post-Nicene Fathers*.

## ABBREVIATIONS

| | |
|---|---|
| Christophilopoulos | A. Χριστοφιλόπουλος. Ἑλληνικὸν ἐκκλησιαστικὸν δίκαιον [Greek Ecclesiastical Law], 3 vols. Athens: Ἐκδοτικὸς Οἶκος Δημ. Ν. Τζάκα-Στεφ. Δελαγραμμάτικα, 1954–1956. |
| Milaš | Ν. Μίλας. Τὸ ἐκκλησιαστικὸν δίκαιον τῆς Ὀρθοδόξου Ἀνατολικῆς Ἐκκλησίας [The Ecclesiastical Law of the EasternOrthodoxChurch],trans.,Μ.Ἀποστολόπουλος. Athens, Τύποις Π. Δ. Σακελλαρίου, 1906. |
| Mouratides | Κ. Μουρατίδης. Κανονικὸν δίκαιον [Canon Law]. Athens, 1960. |
| Percival | H. Percival, ed. The Seven Ecumenical Councils, vol. 14, Nicene and Post-Nicene Fathers, second series. Grand Rapids, MI: Eerdmans, 1956. |
| Rhallēs and Potlēs | Γ.Α. Ῥάλλης and Μ. Ποτλῆς. Σύνταγμα θείων καὶ ἱερῶν κανόνων τῶν τε ἁγίων καὶ πανευφήμων ἀποστόλων καὶ τῶν ἱερῶν οἰκουμενικῶν καὶ τοπικῶν συνόδων καὶ τῶν κατὰ μέρος ἁγίων πατέρων [Collection of the Divine and Holy Canons of Both the Holy and Wholly Blessed Apostles, the Sacred Ecumenical and Local Synods and the Individual Holy Fathers], 6 vols. Athens: Γ. Χαρτοφύλαξ, 1852–1859. |
| Rodopoulos | P. Rodopoulos. An Overview of Orthodox Canon Law. Rollinsford, NH: Orthodox Research Institute, 2007. |
| Rudder | Agapios Hieromonk and Nikodēmos Monk. The Rudder (Pedalion) of the Metaphorical Ship of the One Holy Catholic and Apostolic Church of the Orthodox Christians, trans., D. Cummings. Chicago: The Orthodox Christian Educational Society, 1983. |
| Trempelas | Παναγιώτης Τρεμπέλας. Μικρὸν εὐχολόγιον [Small Euchologion], 2 vols. Athens: n.p., 1950, 1955. |

## GENERAL PRINCIPLES

Canon law is a discipline that incorporates legal methods to apply the theology of the Church to her daily life. In this sense, canon law is the discipline that seeks to bridge the gulf between the ideal model of Christian life and the reality of the struggle in which the Church exists. As such, the study of canon law presupposes a full understanding of two concepts: law (νόμος) and church (Ἐκκλησία). It is the purpose of canon law to harmonize these two concepts in a way that addresses the needs of the Church as it exists in, but not of, the world. Although the concept of church may be familiar to those who study theology, that of law may not. One may also find it difficult to distinguish between law and ethics; consequently, this distinction must be addressed from the outset of the study of canon law.

### DEFINITIONS

#### LAW

Law and ethics are constitutive principles that regulate human relationships. The principles of ethics have a wider field of application than those of law because they regulate a broader set of interactions. Ethics regulate the relations of an individual to

God, oneself, and others. They are concerned primarily with inner disposition, whereas the principles of law are concerned primarily with the behavior that results from such a disposition. The commandments "You shall not murder" and "You shall not steal" are examples of law, whereas the origins of the actions prohibited—covetousness and anger respectively—are the concern of ethics (Exod 20:13, 15).[1] Yet while law and ethics may be distinguished from one another, they can never be fully separated. On the contrary, they are considered a unity through which moral order in the world is regulated for the benefit of all.

It must be emphasized, however, that law almost inevitably involves an element of coercion that is absent from ethics. It is the sum total of the compulsory rules that regulate our behavior with the goal of harmonious relationships.[2] There are two main divisions of law as we apply it within the Church: divine law and human law. Divine law encompasses both positive law (the Decalogue) and natural law (conscience). Human law encompasses both written law and custom. It is the purpose of canon law to understand and combine these various forms into an amalgam that addresses the needs of the Church and her faithful.

## CHURCH ('Εκκλησία)

The Church is a great mystery and defies simple definition. She is the mystical body of Christ, of which Christ himself is the head. She is the reflection of Christ's dual nature (his hypostatic union), both human and divine. She is the visible organization of the Kingdom of God, the assembly in which the people of God find communion with him. She is this and more.

She is, indeed, an organization. And because she is a human organization, the Church requires laws to regulate the harmonious relationships of her members and the realization of her purpose—

---

1 Christ himself draws such a distinction when he says: "You have heard that it was said to those of old, '*You shall not murder,* and whoever murders will be in danger of the judgment.' But I say to you that whoever is angry with his brother without a cause shall be in danger of the judgment" (Matt 5:21–22).

2 In contrast to this understanding of law, the spirit of the canons is fundamentally compassionate. See Appendix B: "The Spirit of Compassion in the Canonical Tradition of the Church."

their salvation. Yet while she is a human organization, which outwardly resembles other worldly organizations, the source of her being is God. The principle means by which the visible, human element of the Church is united with her invisible, divine element are the sacraments of baptism, Eucharist, and priesthood. These and other institutions of the Church have as their ultimate purpose the union of the members of the visible Church with her invisible head, Jesus Christ. A person's dual nature—human and spiritual—requires that the Church employ corresponding means (rules of law) to effect salvation. The ultimate goal of law within the Church is the salvation of humanity.

The divine element of the Church is her life-giving source, just as the spirit gives life to the body. In this way, the human element is subordinate to the divine. Yet the human element should never be overlooked. The Church requires the coordination of her members, just as a properly functioning body does (1 Cor 12:12-31). The divine and human elements of the Church are united harmoniously, indivisibly, and without confusion as they are in the incarnate Christ. In this way, the mystery of the Church reflects the mystery of the dual nature of Christ. Neither the mystery of the incarnation nor the mystery of the Church can be perfectly defined. Due to the supernatural character of the Church and the limitations of human reason, we must resort to a descriptive definition. We have in Scripture a wealth of examples and illustrations to aid in this quest.

In the gospel of Saint Matthew, the Church is God's kingdom on earth (Matt 16:18) and a visible organization (Matt 18:15-17). Elsewhere in the Gospels, she is referred to as the "kingdom of God" (Matt 12:28, Mark 1:15, Luke 4:43, John 3:3) and "kingdom of heaven" (Matt 3:2, 5:3, 8:11).[3] In Acts, the Epistles and Revelation, she is defined as "all who believe in Christ" (Acts 11:26, 14:23, 27; Rom 16:4, 16),[4] the Christians of a local church (in Jerusalem, Acts 8:1; in Corinth, 1 Cor 1:2, 16:1; in Rome, Rev 1:4), or the church in the home (Rom 16:5, 1 Cor 16:19, Col 4:15).[5]

---

3 Mouratides, 16–17.

4 See also: 1 Cor 4:17, 6:4; 2 Cor 8:18, 23, 24; Rev 1:20, 2:7, 23.

5 Mouratides, 17.

In his work on the canons, Mouratides called the early Church the "new people of God," underscoring her supernatural character, stemming from baptism.[6] He further describes the Church as the people of God living in hierarchical order for the purpose of realizing the kingdom of God on earth.[7] The term "hierarchical" refers to ἱερὰ ἀρχή (divine source) and ἱερὰ ἐξουσία (divine authority). In this sense, the divine source of the Church is to be found in the unfathomable will of God, while divine authority is what allows the Church to fulfill her purpose, which is humanity's salvation.

Expressions of God's will for the creation of the visible Church are found in the call of the disciples, the selection of the twelve, the sending of the disciples and apostles to evangelize, the institution of baptism and the Eucharist, the granting of authority, and the adoption of the fundamental precepts of governing the Church.

Based on the above, the Church is defined as the divine-human institution founded by our Lord Jesus Christ for the salvation and sanctification of the faithful and is guided by the Holy Spirit to achieve this end. She is composed of all who correctly believe in Christ as God and Savior and are united organically by the same Orthodox faith and sacraments into one *body* with the Lord as *head*. She is distinguished into clergy (κλῆρος), who are consecrated through the sacrament of ordination, and laity (λαός). She is administered by bishops, who trace their origin from the apostles by continual succession, and through them to the Lord Jesus Christ himself.[8]

This definition concerns the visible Church, or Church militant (*Ecclesia militans*), and the invisible Church, or Church triumphant (*Ecclesia triumphans*). Both these elements of the Church constitute a single, organic whole. Aspects of the visible Church are her living members, the hierarchy, and the sacraments. Aspects of the invisible Church are her head (Jesus Christ), her deceased members, and divine grace.

---

6 Mouratides, 17.

7 Mouratides, 18, based on Eduard Eichmann and Klaus Mörsdorf, *Lehrbuch des Kirchenrechts auf Grund des Codex Iuris Canonici*, 10th ed. (Paderborn: Verlag Ferdinand Schöningh, 1959), 1:24–27.

8 Mouratides, 21. See also Appendix B: "Lived Experience and Theoretical Differences," 185–186.

## CHURCH AND LAW

The visible Church is the organized community of faithful governed by canons. Jesus Christ became man in order to free humanity from the formalism of law and guide it to the spirit of freedom and love, and the Church is reconciled to this teaching through her sacraments and canons. The Church utilizes these means to achieve her lofty purpose. Although the Church is simultaneously a human and a divine institution, her earthly organization is predominantly spiritual. As long as the Church, as Church militant, possesses her earthly form of being, canons must constitute the external means of security within which the free life of the Spirit is developed. Consequently, even in her visible form, the structure of the Church militant is predominantly spiritual. While her canonical tradition constitutes an external means of security, it also allows the visible Church militant to reflect the invisible Church triumphant.

## CANON LAW

Before proceeding to a definition of the academic term "canon law," it will prove helpful to examine the significance of the Greek word κανών (kanōn) from which it derives. Literally, κανών is the stem of a reed—an item that was often used in ancient times as a measuring stick. Metaphorically, it is a model or prototype. In ecclesiastical terminology it has two meanings: the authentic list of books of Holy Scripture, or a decree of ecclesiastical law promulgated by a synod.[9] In the strict sense, within the Orthodox Church, canon law is the system of law contained in the collection of laws and canons known as the *Nomokanon in 14 Titles* (Ὁ Νομοκάνων εἰς 14 τίτλους) compiled in several forms with its final edition in the eleventh century.

---

9 These canons include patristic texts received as having canonical authority, such as the canons of Saint Basil the Great.

With this in mind, canon law is defined as the sum of canons and canonical decrees deriving from the Church on her own authority. The life of the Church is governed by them, especially her organization and her relations to her members, to those outside her fold, to the state, and to other religious or secular bodies. The ultimate purpose of all canonical sources promulgated by the Church for her members is their salvation.[10]

There are several divisions of canon law. With regard to its source, it is either of divine origin based on Scripture, or of human origin derived in synods (the former is unchangeable, whereas the latter is not). Another division may be made between written law, which is promulgated by a legislative body, and unwritten law, which is adopted by custom. Internal law, which regulates life within the Church, can be distinguished from external law, which regulates the relations of the Church with the state and other bodies outside her sphere. There is also a distinction between canon law and ecclesiastical law. Ecclesiastical law includes all the rules of law adopted by both Church and state regulating the affairs of the Church. As such, ecclesiastical law is broader in scope than canon law, although in practice both pertain to the Church.

## RELATED FIELDS

The importance of canon law is seen in its maintenance of the administrative order of the Church, and in its influence on society—the field of law in particular. Practically all branches of law have been influenced by canon law.[11] In fact, the influence of canon law has had a mitigating effect on the severity of European legal thought beginning in the distant past. Two telling examples are the humanization of criminal law and the law of debt after Christianity became the official religion of the Roman Empire. Contrary to the earlier secular practice of penalizing offenses indiscriminately, the principles of canon law required consideration of intent and context, and the exercise of leniency when warranted. Consequently, canon law has contributed not only to the progress of European legal

---

10  Mouratides, 24; see also Rodopoulos, 20–22.
11  Mouratides, 49–55.

thought over the centuries, but also to the progress of Western civilization in general.[12]

The term "canon law" might be more properly understood as "canonical tradition."[13] Though it does bear a certain similarity to secular jurisprudence, canon law is derived from its own, independent sources. The origins of these sources are found in the will of Jesus Christ to establish his kingdom on earth. Canon law, therefore, is not subject to any of the distinctions of secular law, such as civil law, criminal law, or corporate law.

Like jurisprudence, canon law has all of the external characteristics common to secular law: persons invested with authority and the means of promulgation, formulation, interpretation, application, validation, amendment, and abolition of law. Canon law, however, unlike secular law, gathers its material from theology and systematizes it through the legal method. Because of its association with both jurisprudence and theology, canon law is said to have two foci. It differs from secular law in cause (predisposition), purpose (salvation), origin (divine), and extent (timeless). Hence, the law of the Church is primarily spiritual and sacred. As such, it concerns itself with the inner disposition behind every act or neglect thereof.

Unlike secular law, or even Mosaic law, where legalism may appear in the distribution of justice, the Church's law through God's grace pursues its own purpose: the spiritual perfection of the Church's members. This purpose is the determining factor in the authority granted to apply the law according to each individual case. The spirit of love, reflected in commitment to the spiritual perfection of the individual, must prevail in the law's application. Interpretation of the letter of the law by its spirit gave way to the institution of *oikonomia* (*οἰκονομία*).[14] Through *oikonomia*, the legal consequences following violation of the law are lifted for the benefit of both the law's transgressor and the church body. The spiritual character of canon law is thereby evident from the fact

---

12 Mouratides, 54–55.

13 See Appendix B: "The Canonical Tradition of the Orthodox Church," 137.

14 For an in-depth investigation of *oikonomia* and an accompanying bibliography, see Appendix B: "The Application of *Oikonomia*: The Experience of the Orthodox Church in America."

that it is not coercive as is secular law. The purpose of the Church's authority is service to others, whereas the purpose of the state's authority is sovereignty over others.

There is much interaction between canon law and other theological disciplines, and the study and integration of these parallel fields aid in a comprehensive interpretation of the canons. The study and interpretation of the Old and New Testaments assist in understanding the fundamental source of canon law, Holy Scripture. Church history offers insights concerning conditions under which canons were adopted and applied. Dogmatics is related, since many of the topics of canon law, such as the sacraments of initiation into the Church (baptism and chrismation), also enter the realm of dogma. Ethics can be considered together with canon law to constitute a unified element. Patrology is relevant, since the writings of many church Fathers were used in the formation of canon law. Liturgics and pastoral theology both express how theology is lived and experienced. Aspects of all these theological disciplines underlie the canons and affect the way in which they are understood.

Similarly, canon law is related to several fields of jurisprudence. Philosophy of law affords a familiarization with the principles and ideals of law. Historically, Greco-Roman law influenced canon law in its institutions of administration and law of procedure, whereas canon law influenced Greco-Roman law in its essence and content (e.g., asserting individual rights, and humanizing criminal law and the law of debt). Judaic law has some overlap since some decrees of Mosaic law were introduced into canon law. Secular law is the law of each land where the Church exists.[15]

## METHODS OF STUDY AND INTERPRETATION

Several methods are employed in the examination of canon law. The empirical method interprets the canons by the way they are applied. The historical method studies the canons in the context of their origins, historical development, and application. The philosophical or critical method examines the canons in their

---

15  Mouratides, 55–56.

relationship with each other, law in general, logic, nature, and the purpose of the Church. The historical-philosophical method combines the previous two methods. Lastly, the historical-theological method combines the historical method and the study of the theological content of the canons. This method is most preferable, because it respects the meaning and purpose of the canons in their original theological context while seeking to apply them in the present.

In order to avoid error in the application of law, it must be correctly understood. A merely technical knowledge of the law can be deceiving. What is necessary is an understanding of the spirit of the law. This can only be attained by understanding *the legislator's purpose for issuing the law.* Discovery of this purpose is the goal of interpretation. Several contexts must be kept in mind when attempting interpretation: grammatical, logical, historical, systematic, and spiritual.

*Grammatical* interpretation has as its objective the letter of the law. It consists of interpreting words and expressions inserted in the text of the law by the legislator. *Logical* interpretation examines the logical relationship of the various components of the law to each other. *Historical* interpretation investigates the origin of the law and the situation that led to its promulgation. *Systematic* interpretation refers to the inner relationship of the law with other laws. In order to understand the law fully, it is necessary to determine its relationship to the general system of law. Finally, as an expression of the Holy Spirit, which lives within the Church, the holy canons must be interpreted *by the Spirit,* through which they have their being.[16]

Although no standardized division of canon law exists, there are two commonly used alternatives.[17] In the first division, the material of canon law is classified according to the three offices of our Lord

---

16 Ἰ. Κοτσώνης, Σημειώσεις κανονικοῦ δικαίου τῆς Ὀρθοδόξου Ἀνατολικῆς Ἐκκλησίας [*Canon Law Notes of the Eastern Orthodox Church*], 3 vols. (Thessaloniki: n.p., 1960–1962), 1:74. For instances of canonical opinions based on interpretation of the canons, see Appendix B: "*Miscellanea Canonica*: Responses to Canonical Irregularities."

17 These two different approaches are reflected in the works cited above of Κοτσώνης and Milaš.

as king, priest, and prophet, and to their corresponding authorities (administrative, priestly, and magisterial). In the second, which is the division used for this present work, the material of canon law is classified according to the following general categories:

- Sources

- Ecclesiastical polity

- Administration

- Life of the Church

- Relations of the Church to the state and to non-Orthodox Christians[18]

---

18 Owing to the practical purpose for which *Introduction to Orthodox Canon Law* was written, the category "relations of the Church to the state and to non-Orthodox Christians" has been omitted. "Relations of the Church to the state" does not correspond to the principle of separation of church and state that applies to the Church in America. It has been replaced by the topic "Governance of the Local Church." "Relations of the Church to non-Orthodox Christians" has been addressed by a reflection on "Orthodoxy and Ecumenism" and reproduction of a pertinent section of the publication *Guidelines for Orthodox Christians in Ecumenical Relations*, found in Appendix A.

# I. SOURCES OF CANON LAW

The source of all law within the Church is the will of God. From this source stem both ecclesiastical legislation and ecclesiastical custom. When speaking of sources, one must keep in mind the distinction between primary sources and secondary sources. In the context of canon law, primary sources are the actual canons and laws themselves. Secondary sources are the texts through which we learn of precedents or law applied at a particular place and time, such as legal works, judicial decisions, documents, and information generally contained in non-legal works.

The sources of canon law, in order of importance, are fundamental, historical, and practical. Fundamental sources are those sources that are the basis of the entire discipline. Scripture, holy tradition, canons, and ecclesiastical decrees pertaining to the universal Church are contained in this category. Historical sources, on the other hand, include laws of the state based on canons. The nomokanons—collections of ecclesiastical laws and corresponding canons related to ecclesiastical matters—belong to this category as well. Practical sources include statutory charters and regulations of local churches.

The sources of canon law are divided into four main periods. The first period extends from the institution of the Church to the First Ecumenical Council held in Nicea in the year 325. During this period, the Church suffered intermittent persecution. The second period extends from the First Ecumenical Council to the Schism of

867 between the Eastern and Western Churches. The third period extends from the Schism of 867 to the fall of Constantinople in 1453. The fourth period extends from the fall of Constantinople to the present.[19]

## 1.1 SOURCES OF THE FIRST PERIOD (INSTITUTION OF THE CHURCH TO 325)

### HOLY SCRIPTURE

Holy Scripture is the primary written monument of the first period and the most important source of information about the Christian faith. In it are commands issued by our Lord and understood as laws. As such, they are eternal, unalterable, and irrevocable. They are valid and normative for the entire Church and constitute its fundamental law. Chief among them are ordinances concerning stewardship of the apostles, relations of the apostles to each other, baptism, the Eucharist, marriage, and oaths.[20]

There are also laws adopted by the apostles based on our Lord's authority. Such laws belong to the same category as scriptural laws. They address issues concerning the ordination and appointment of presbyters, qualifications and obligations of the elders of the Church, and sustenance of the clergy.[21] Furthermore, there are legal precepts of the Old Testament that are valid only if they have been adopted by Christian sources. Such an example is the general prohibition of lending at interest (Deut 23:20–21), which applies only to clerics based on several early canons.[22]

---

19 Mouratides, 58–59; see also Christophilopoulos, 1:16–17.

20 Stewardship, Matt 18:18, John 20:23; relations among apostles, Mark 9:34–35; baptism, Matt 28:19, Mark 16:16, John 3:5; Eucharist, Luke 22:19, 1 Cor 11:23–25; marriage, Matt 5:32, 19:3; oaths, Matt 5:33–36.

21 Presbyters, Acts 14:23, Titus 1:5; obligations of elders, 1 Tim 3:2–7, 4:14, 5:22; 2 Tim 1:6, Titus 1:6–9, 1 Pet 5:2–3; sustenance of clergy, 1 Cor 9:6–7, 1 Tim 5:17–18.

22 Holy Apostles 44, 1 Nicea 17, Trullo 10.

## HOLY TRADITION

Holy tradition is the next source in order of precedence belonging to the first period. It is the oral and unwritten teaching of our Lord and the apostles, delivered from mouth to mouth and from generation to generation in unbroken succession. It is preserved in the writings of the Fathers of the first three centuries especially, and in the remaining written monuments of the Church. Holy tradition is the living and abiding presence of the Holy Spirit in the Church in accordance with the promise of Christ. It is the ever-expanding and unfolding embodiment of the phrase "all truth," into which Christ states the Church will be led by the "Spirit of truth" (John 15:26–27, 16:12–13).

The Church has always attached great importance to tradition, recognizing it of equal importance to Scripture, since it is complementary to and confirmed by Holy Scripture. In his second epistle to the Thessalonians, Saint Paul exhorts: "Stand fast and hold the traditions which you were taught, whether by word or our epistle" (2 Thess 2:15). The importance of holy tradition is also repeatedly emphasized throughout the canons of the Church. The First Ecumenical Council of Nicea (325) refers to ancient tradition and commands: "Let the ancient customs (in Egypt, Libya, and Pentapolis) prevail."[23] The Council of Gangra (340) states: "We wish that all things which have been delivered by the Holy Scriptures and the Apostolic traditions, may be observed in the Church."[24] Indeed, holy tradition is so important that the Council in Trullo (691–692)[25] asserts: "If any bishop or presbyter shall not perform . . . according to what has been handed down by the Apostles . . . let him be deposed, as innovating upon the things which have been handed down."[26]

---

23 1 Nicea 6; see also canon 7 of the same council.
24 Gangra 21.
25 The Council in Trullo, having completed the disciplinary work of the Fifth and Sixth Ecumenical Councils with its 102 canons, is also known as the Penthektē (Fifth-Sixth) Council in Greek sources and the Quinisext Concilium in Latin sources. Its ecumenical character has always been recognized by the Orthodox Church.
26 Trullo 32.

## CUSTOM

The third source of the first period—custom—is, to a certain degree, related to holy tradition. Custom and tradition are similar in that they are both unwritten law, yet they differ significantly. Custom is the consistent and long-standing conviction of the ecclesiastical community pertaining to law concerning a certain act. Two things are necessary for the acceptance of custom: there must be a long and steady practice, and there must be a consensus of opinion that the custom has the force of law. In order for custom to be accepted as a source of canon law, it must not be contrary to any doctrine of Orthodox faith and must be in absolute agreement with Holy Scripture and holy tradition. With regard to local or special custom, it must not in any way be opposed to the general spirit of canon law or Christian ethics.

Because of the absence of an official codification of Orthodox canon law similar to the *Codex Iuris Canonici* of the Roman Catholic Church, custom plays an important practical role in filling the lacunae of Orthodox ecclesiastical legislation. There are two types of customs: universal and local. Universal customs are those practiced throughout the entire Orthodox Church; local customs are only practiced locally. These may be further divided into two categories: general and special. General customs apply to all members of the Church; special customs apply only to certain members of the Church (e.g., monks). Local customs prevail over universal and special customs over general.

## ANONYMOUS CODIFIED WORKS

A fourth source of the first period is a collection of anonymous codified works of apostolic tradition. It includes the *Didache*, the *Didaskalia*, and the *Ecclesiastical Canons of the Holy Apostles*. The *Didache* is a brief work dating back to the primitive Church (end of the first or beginning of the second century). Therein lies its importance, for it reveals details regarding her worship, life, and polity. The *Didaskalia* is a similarly informative work probably composed in Syria and dating to the first or second half of the third century. The original Greek source is lost but has been preserved in Syriac and partially in Latin translation. The *Ecclesiastical Canons* of the Holy Apostles, not to be confused with the eighty-five *Apostolic Canons* to be mentioned later, is another brief work most likely composed in Egypt during the beginning of the fourth century. Its original Greek source has been preserved, as have translations in several ancient languages.

## REGIONAL COUNCILS

A fifth source of the first period is a number of canons of two regional councils ratified by the *Penthektē* Ecumenical Council in Trullo. They are the Councils of Ancyra in 314, with twenty-five canons, and Neocaesarea (ca. 315), with fifteen canons. Among their canons, two deserve special mention. Canon 10 of Ancyra permits the marriage of a deacon after ordination, provided that the candidate makes known his intention beforehand. This canon eventually fell into disuse; nevertheless, it could very well form the basis for future discussions concerning the validity of marriage after ordination.[27] Canon 11 of Neocaesarea determines the age of ordination for presbyters at thirty, for at this age our Lord began his public ministry. This canon, too, has fallen into disuse.

## CHURCH FATHERS

A sixth source of the first period is a number of canons of three Fathers of the third and early fourth centuries. These are four of Dionysios of Alexandria (d. 265), eleven of Gregory of Neocaesarea (d. 270),[28] and fifteen of Peter of Alexandria (d. 311). Generally, these were written due to the relative scarcity of ecclesiastical legislation during the early centuries of the Church. The Fathers filled this omission by writing their opinions on various canonical questions, recording a living tradition within the Church of their time. It is important to remember, however, that their opinions were often written in response to specific questions put to them directly, and thus are frequently pastoral in nature. Although they originate locally in different ecclesial centers, they are recognized as universally applicable.

---

27 It is, however, still upheld by the Ethiopian (Oriental) Orthodox.
28 The number of canons of Saint Gregory of Neocaesarea in Rhallēs and Potlēs is 11, and in the *Rudder* 12.

## 1.2 SOURCES OF THE SECOND PERIOD (325–867)

### ECUMENICAL COUNCILS

During the second period, which extends to the Schism of 867, the ecumenical councils emerge. Hierarchically, an ecumenical council is the highest ecclesiastical body exercising supreme administrative, judicial, and especially legislative authority. The work of these councils consists primarily of defining dogma and formulating canons. This period also saw the rise of the See of Constantinople.

The First Ecumenical Council of Nicea, summoned in 325 by the emperor Constantine to deal with the trinitarian controversy, promulgated twenty canons. These dealt with the aftermath of the great persecution of Diocletian, the reception of those who had lapsed from the faith, the structure of the Church, and the conduct of the clergy. The remaining ecumenical councils followed suit, each with its own issues to address: 1 Constantinople in 381with seven canons, Ephesus in 431 with eight canons, Chalcedon in 451 with thirty canons, 2 Constantinople in 553 and 3 Constantinople in 680 (both without canons), the Council in Trullo (*Penthektē*) in 692 with 102 canons, and 2 Nicea in 787 with twenty-two canons.

The Second Ecumenical Council of Constantinople is best known for its role in halting the further spread of heresy regarding the second and third persons of the Holy Trinity. Canon 3 of this council places the See of Constantinople second in rank after the See of Rome among the five main ecclesiastical centers of Christianity. The Third Ecumenical Council of Ephesus addressed the issue related to the two natures of Christ, declaring them divine and human. Canon 8 of this council recognized the autocephaly of the Church of Cyprus. The Fourth Ecumenical Council of Chalcedon further clarified the doctrine of the two natures of Christ. Its canon 28 accords the bishop of Constantinople the same primacy of honor given the bishop of Rome.

The Fifth and Sixth Ecumenical Councils were exclusively preoccupied with doctrinal matters, the Fifth with lingering Nestorian sentiments and the Sixth with the doctrine regarding the two wills of Christ. In the absence of canonical decrees by these two councils, the *Penthektē* Ecumenical Council in Trullo repaired this omission. As its name implies, it continued their work and issued only canons, thereby adopting the greatest number of canons among the seven ecumenical councils. This council is regarded as an extension of the Sixth Ecumenical Council. Canon 2 is especially noteworthy in that together with the canons of all previous ecumenical councils, it ratified the eighty-five *Apostolic Canons*, the canons of certain regional councils, and those of several Fathers. By doing so, it granted them universal authority. The Seventh Ecumenical Council met to end the iconoclastic controversy. Its canon 9 is a stern admonition to those who conceal writings of the iconoclasts against sacred images. Canon 1 ratified the canons of the previous six ecumenical councils.

## REGIONAL COUNCILS

In addition to the ecumenical councils, there are also the canons of regional councils from this period ratified by canon 2 of the Council of Trullo. Among them are the Councils of Gangra (ca. 340) with twenty canons, Antioch in 341 with twenty-five canons, Laodicea (between 343 and 381) with sixty canons, and Constantinople (394) with two canons. The Council of Gangra convened to deal with the confusion caused by the ascetic zeal of the Eustathians. Several of its canons elevate the status of marriage, under attack by the Eustathians, to a level consonant with the Church's corresponding theology of marriage. The Council of Antioch concerned itself with doctrinal matters related to the Arian controversy. Its canons, addressing the all-important issues of ecclesiastical order and administration, were widely acclaimed in both East and West. Having as their primary source the canons of the First Ecumenical Council, the canons of the Council of Laodicea are for the most part of ethical and liturgical content. Among the many councils that met in Constantinople, the regional council of 394 deserves special mention: it issued two canons forbidding two or three bishops to dethrone another bishop. This is a decision that can only be reached by all bishops of the province since all bishops share in the same hierarchical authority.

Besides the above councils, which were convened in the eastern part of the Roman Empire, there were councils held in the western part as well. These include the Councils of Sardica (ca. 343) with twenty-one canons, Carthage in 251 (at the time of Cyprian) with one canon, and Carthage in 419 with 133 canons. The Council of Sardica, like that of Antioch at about the same time in the East, was concerned with the Arian controversy. It was concerned as well with attacks against Saint Athanasios. Its canons were not immediately accepted in the East due to the preponderance of Western bishops in attendance, as well as to the recognized right of appeal to the bishop of Rome. While the Council of Carthage held in 251 belongs to the sources of the first period, it is included here among other councils held in the West. It issued one canon referring to the rejection of the baptism of heretics. The Council of Carthage held in 419 reaffirmed the 121 canons of previous regional councils held in Carthage and promulgated twelve new canons, thereby creating the collection known as *The Canonical Code of the African Church*.[29]

## CHURCH FATHERS

There are canons of the Fathers from this period as well. In the late fourth century, there were three canons attributed to Athanasios the Great (d. 373). They deal with issues of purity, the canon of Scripture, and the Arian controversy. Ninety-two canons are attributed to Basil the Great (d. 379), created for the most part from his epistles and treatise on the Holy Spirit. Eighteen canonical answers to questions by various bishops and presbyters concerning matters of ecclesiastical concern are ascribed to Timothy of Alexandria (d. 385). The poetic writings of Gregory the Theologian (d. 389) regarding the number of canonical books of Holy Scripture comprise a canon. Also, sixty-nine verses of a poem concerning the books of Holy Scripture are ascribed to Amphilochios of Iconium (d. 395) as a canon. Finally, eight canons are derived from an epistle written by Gregory of Nyssa (d. 394).

Following the fourth century, there are canons from several other eminent Fathers as well. Theophilos of Alexandria (d. 412)

---

29 The enumeration of these canons varies in some collections as well. In Rhallēs and Potlēs, used for this study, the number is fixed at 133 and in the *Rudder* at 141.

wrote extensively about Theophany and topics of disciplinary concern. From these writings there are fourteen canons. Five canons are attributed to Cyril of Alexandria (d. 444) from two of his epistles. An encyclical letter was composed by Gennadios of Constantinople (d. 471) and accepted as a canon. It was addressed to all metropolitans and to the Pope of Rome concerning simony. Much later, Tarasios of Constantinople (d. 809) composed an epistle on simony to Pope Hadrian.[30] This, too, was accepted as a canon.

## MONASTIC CANONS

There are also monastic canons. These differ from general canons in that they are designed to apply only to monastics. Most important among them are the canons of Pachomios (d. 346), the founder of coenobitic monasticism, and those of Basil the Great (d. 379). Although these canons were not ratified by an ecumenical council, the prestige of their compilers assured their universal acceptance. Canons falsely attributed to Nikēphoros of Constantinople (d. 829) also lack ratification by an ecumenical council, although they are nevertheless included in many canonical collections. In addition, there are collections of penances to be imposed upon lay penitents by their spiritual fathers falsely ascribed to outstanding ecclesiastical personalities such as Athanasios the Great (d. 373), John Chrysostom (d. 407), and John the Faster (d. 595).[31]

## ANONYMOUS CODIFIED WORKS

Anonymous codified works belonging to this period are the *Apostolic Constitutions*, the *Epitome of Book VIII of the Apostolic Constitutions*, the *Testament of our Lord*, and the *Canons of Hippolytus*. The *Apostolic Constitutions* is the most significant anonymous codified work of this period. Written around the end of the fourth or beginning of the fifth century in Syria, it is composed of eight books based on the *Didaskalia* (Books I–VI), the *Didache* (Book VII), and the *Apostolic Tradition of Hippolytus* (most of Book VIII). Chapter 47 of Book VIII contains the eighty-five *Apostolic Canons*, the only part of the work

---

30 For additional discussion of simony, see the sections below dealing with "Qualifications of an Ordaining Hierarch"; "Election, Ordination, and Affirmation of Bishops"; and "Ecclesiastical Offenses."

31 Mouratides, 81–82.

ratified by Canon 2 of the *Penthektē* Ecumenical Council in Trullo. It rejected the remainder of the work as falsified by heretics.

Of less significance are the *Epitome of Book VIII of the Apostolic Constitutions*, the *Testament of our Lord*, and the *Canons of Hippolytus*. The *Testament of our Lord*, based on the *Apostolic Tradition of Hippolytus*, was written within monophysitic circles of Syria during the second half of the fifth century. Similarly, the so-called *Canons of Hippolytus*, dating from about the year 500, are based on the same *Apostolic Tradition*.[32]

## STATE LEGISLATION

During the second period, a new phenomenon emerged: the participation of the state in ecclesiastical affairs. Consequently, for the first time there appear canonical sources emanating from the state. First among them is the *Codex Theodosianus*, composed in 438 during the reign of Theodosius II and Valentinian III.[33] It includes all state legislation concerning the Church from the time of Constantine the Great. Next in chronological order, and of considerable importance, is the *Corpus Iuris Civilis* of Justinian (527–569). Composed of the *Codex Justinianus, Digestae, Institutiones,* and *Novellae Constitutiones*, it became the standard source of Roman law and the authoritative manifestation of its influence. Following is the *Ecloga* of Leo III the Isaurian (717–741), whose intention it was to combine the most important legislation from the four collections of Justinian into a single code. The *Procheiros Nomos* is a manual of eastern Roman law published by Emperor Basil I, possibly between 870 and 879. The *Epanagoge* is another legal code of the same emperor compiled around 879. The *Basilika* of Leo VI the Wise (886–912) was considered the official legal code for the Empire, which was begun under the emperor Basil I (867–886) and completed around 892. Out of the state-produced canonical sources listed here, it is the most important for the canon law of the Orthodox Church. Finally, in addition to the *Novellae Constitutiones*

---

32  Mouratides, 82–83; see also Christophilopoulos, 1:25–26.

33  Up until at least the time of Justinian (sixth century), the administrative documents of the Eastern Roman Empire were written in Latin. This explains their Latin names as well as the frequent use of Latin terms in Orthodox canon law.

("Novels") of Justinian mentioned above, many of these novels regulating ecclesiastical matters were issued by other emperors, particularly by Heraclius (610–641).[34]

## 1.3 SOURCES OF THE THIRD PERIOD (867–1453)

### REGIONAL COUNCILS

Following the era of the ecumenical councils, the number of sources in the third period declined. Although not numbered among the ecumenical councils, two regional councils occurred related to the controversy involving Patriarchs Ignatius and Photios. These reflected contemporary tensions between the Eastern and Western Churches and are of significant importance. The first is the Council of Constantinople in 861, known as *Prōtodeutera* or First-Second (*Πρωτοδευτέρα*), which adopted seventeen canons. It follows the Seventh Ecumenical Council in the *Rudder*, because of its ecumenical significance. Next in sequence is the Council of Constantinople in 879/880, known as Holy Wisdom (Ἁγία Σοφία). Although acclaimed as a council of ecumenical status, it was not recognized in the West. Nevertheless, its three canons have never ceased to be valid in the Orthodox Church. Both of these councils recognized Photios as the legitimate Patriarch of Constantinople. In Byzantine sources, such as the writings of the twelfth-century canonist Theodore Balsamōn, both these councils are recognized as Ecumenical.

### PATRIARCHAL SYNOD

After the last (Seventh) Ecumenical Council (787), legislative authority was mainly exercised by the Patriarch of Constantinople together with the patriarchal synod, and by the emperor. The Patriarchate of Constantinople assumed this authority for several reasons. The Patriarchal See of Constantinople occupies the rank

---

34 Mouratides, 84–88; see also Christophilopoulos, 1:34–35.

of precedence among the other sees of the East. Furthermore, it remained politically free, while the others were under Muslim authority. The Church of Constantinople was also the Mother Church of all those who had been converted by her missionaries.[35]

For these reasons, the Church of Constantinople often created legislation for the benefit of other sees as well. Such legislation is considered valid for the entire Orthodox Church. Often the primates of sister churches were in attendance at councils convened for the deliberation of important matters. Among these matters was the question of the fourth marriage of Leo VI (the Wise). It was determined that while a third marriage was permitted with certain limitations, a fourth marriage was absolutely forbidden. Similarly, marriage impediments were introduced through the Tome of Patriarch Sisinnios I (997) and betrothal was added to them through the Tome of Patriarch John VIII Xiphilinos (1066). Furthermore, decisions of Patriarchs John IX Agapētos (1115) and Lucas I Chrysovergēs (1157) were also introduced, forbidding clerics and monks to exercise any legal profession or participate in secular affairs in general.[36]

## STATE LEGISLATION

Sources emanating from the state include the *Hexabiblos* of the legal scholar Constantine Armenopoulos, issued in 1345 as a manual of ecclesiastical law including legislation on marriage. In addition, there were novels addressing ecclesiastical matters issued by Emperors Leo VI (866–912), Alexios I (1081–1118), Manuel I (1143–1180), and Andronicos II (1282–1328).[37]

## COMMENTARIES

The interpretive works of commentators were also a significant factor during this period. Although there have been many distinguished ecclesiastical writers throughout the centuries, the most renowned writers of canonical works flourished during the twelfth century. Alexios Aristēnos (d. ca. 1166), John Zōnaras (d. ca.

---

35  See Appendix B: "The Primacy of the See of Constantinople in Theory and Practice," 250–52.

36  Mouratides, 89–92; see also Christophilopoulos, 1:30–31.

37  Mouratides, 93.

1159), and Theodore Balsamōn (d. ca. 1195) were the most influential. Alexios Aristēnos, as deacon, ascended to several distinguished offices in the patriarchal court of Constantinople leading ultimately to that of *megas oikonomos*. His synoptic commentary on an abbreviated version of the canons is characteristic of his interpretive methodology. John Zōnaras, for his part, occupied several prominent positions in the government hierarchy. Late in life, he became a monk. His interpretation of the canons, from a complete version, seeks to understand their inner meaning. Therein lies his important contribution to the science of canon law. Theodore Balsamōn entered the ranks of the clergy quite early, serving throughout his career in various clerical offices, including that of Patriarch of Antioch. He is best known for his efforts to harmonize the prescriptions of the canons with the decrees of civil law.[38] Almost a century and a half later, in 1335, the hieromonk Matthew Blastarēs wrote his popular nomokanon, the Σύνταγμα κατὰ στοιχεῖον (*Alphabetical Collection*), a canon law encyclopedia which was divided into twenty-four parts corresponding to the letters of the Greek alphabet. Canons and political laws pertaining to the Church are grouped under headings assigned to each letter.[39]

## 1.4 SOURCES OF THE FOURTH PERIOD (1453–PRESENT)

After the fall of Constantinople and the subjugation of the Greek people, a new situation arose for the Church. Although the Byzantine Empire had fallen, the Church was allowed to exist with a certain amount of freedom. There are two main reasons why the Ottoman Turks were tolerant toward the Church. Firstly, they tolerated the practice of other religions, since their sacred book, the Koran, was applicable only to Muslims. The Koran constituted both their religious and secular code of law. Secondly, they wished

---

38 For a study of Balsamōn, see Patrick Viscuso, *Guide for a Church under Islām: The Sixty-Six Canonical Questions Attributed to Theodōros Balsamōn* (Brookline, MA: Holy Cross Orthodox Press, 2014).

39 Mouratides, 94–95; see also the study and partial translation of Patrick Viscuso, *Sexuality, Marriage, and Celibacy in Byzantine Law: The Alphabetical Collection of Matthew Blastarēs* (Brookline, MA: Holy Cross Orthodox Press, 2008); compare also Milaš, 258–60.

to discourage contact with the West, and therefore permitted many privileges to those churchmen who opposed union with the Western Church. These privileges included free worship, special status and tax exemption for the ecumenical patriarch and bishops, administration of ecclesiastical property by the Church, and the right to exercise authority in family and inheritance law.

In reality, these privileges were not always respected. Extraordinary monetary payments were frequently levied from the Church and great pressure was often exerted on Church leaders to comply with the arbitrary demands of the state. This unpredictable situation existed until the late nineteenth century, when enough pressure was put on the Ottoman government to cease its autocratic method of dealing with minorities. Matters began to improve with the decree *Hatti-Houmayioun*, issued by Sultan Abdul Metzit in 1856. Accordingly, religious freedom for all religions was granted and the equality of all citizens was guaranteed. Christian communities were exempt from paying certain taxes and granted permission to build churches, schools, and philanthropic institutions. Among various other privileges, they also gained the right to attain government posts and serve in civil courts.

Shortly thereafter, the Patriarchate was requested to formulate a statutory charter, which would regulate its organization and administration. Under this statutory charter, known as Ἐθνικοὶ Κανονισμοί (*National Regulations*), the Church of Constantinople retained its autonomy until the Asia Minor Campaign (1919–1922). Following the defeat of the Greek army and the devastating consequences befalling the Greek minority of Asia Minor, the Ecumenical Patriarchate was deprived of the greater part of its flock and limited solely to its religious mission.[40]

During this turbulent period in the history of the Church of Constantinople, from the year 1453 to the present, there are the following sources: patriarchal decrees, synodal decisions, and civil laws pertaining to the Church. The synodal decisions are the most significant.

---

40  Mouratides, 96–98.

## ENDĒMOUSA SYNOD ('Ενδημοῦσα Σύνοδος)

Much of the ecclesiastical legislation of this period originated from what was called an *endēmousa* synod (resident synod). After the fall of the Byzantine Empire, neither ecumenical nor regional councils were convened. As an alternative, the *endēmousa* synod came into existence. It was composed of the ecumenical patriarch, who presided over the assembly, the neighboring bishops of Constantinople, and bishops of the other Eastern patriarchates who were in Constantinople at the time the *endēmousa* synod was convened. Of all bishops attending, those of the suburban sees of Constantinople were most reliably present. These included the sees of Derkon, Chalcedon, Herakleia, and Ephesus. Because of their affinity to the affairs of the Church of Constantinople, the bishops of these four sees were, in essence, the chief administrators of the Patriarchate. This additional distinction earned them the distinguished term γέροντες (venerable elders). Although the *endēmousa* synod is sometimes referred to as a patriarchal synod, it ought not to be confused with the patriarchal synod of the third period that met periodically, while the *endēmousa* synod was a resident synod that met regularly.

When faced with issues of universal importance and concern, the *endēmousa* synod took on a particularly authoritative character. In these proceedings, representatives of other Orthodox Churches were always present. This larger *endēmousa* synod was composed of the twelve hierarchs of the synod of the Church of Constantinople headed by the ecumenical patriarch, the four γέροντες (of Derkon, Chalcedon, Herakleia, and Ephesus), hierarchs sojourning in Constantinople at that time, and other patriarchs of the East (Alexandria, Antioch, and Jerusalem) or their representatives. An *endēmousa* synod at which other patriarchates of the East were not represented was of a more limited scope.

The larger and more representative *endēmousa* synod dealt with a number of serious challenges. These included the issue of Protestant communions seeking relations with the Orthodox Church (1572–1579), rejection of the Gregorian calendar (1580–1584), independence of the Church of Russia and eventual elevation to patriarchal status (1589–1595), acceptance of autocephaly as the form of administration in the Orthodox Church and proclamation of the autocephaly of the Church of Greece (under Anthimos IV; 1848–1852), and recognition of the autocephaly of the Church of Serbia (under Joachim III; 1878–1884).[41]

## 1.5 COLLECTIONS OF CANON LAW

Owing to the importance shared by canons and laws of the state in ecclesiastical practice, both were included in combined collections called nomokanons. There are several collections of canon law worthy of note. The Συναγωγὴ κανόνων εἰς 50 τίτλους (*Collection of Ecclesiastical Canons in 50 Titles*), compiled in the middle of the sixth century by John Scholastikos (later Patriarch of Constantinople), represents the first preserved nomokanon. The Νομοκάνων εἰς 14 τίτλους (*Nomokanon in 14 Titles*), which was once erroneously thought to have been a contribution of Photios the Great (although he may have been involved in one of its revisions), dates back to the first half of the seventh century. There were three editions, the last of which is dated 1090. The fourteen titles of the *Nomokanon* are divided into chapters with topic headings under which related canons and ecclesiastical laws are included. The *Rudder*,[42] a more recent collection dating from 1793, was compiled by the Athonite monks Agapios and Nikodēmos. It has since had several editions and is a very useful collection. A lengthy interpretation appears together with the text of each canon; corresponding related canons are also cited. Appended at the end of the collection are guidelines concerning degrees of relationship and specimens of various types of ecclesiastical letters.

In addition to these, the Σύνταγμα θείων καὶ ἱερῶν κανόνων τῶν τε ἁγίων καὶ πανευφήμων ἀποστόλων καὶ τῶν ἱερῶν οἰκουμενικῶν καὶ τοπικῶν συνόδων καὶ τῶν κατὰ μέρος ἁγίων πατέρων (*Collection of the Divine and Holy Canons of Both the Holy and*

---

41  Mouratides, 98–100.
42  The word "Rudder" is the English translation of "Πηδάλιον." The translation of the work was first published in 1957 and reprinted in 1983. Although its language is archaic and literal, the commentaries accompanying each of the canons by Saint Nikodēmos the Hagiorite, the compiler of the "Πηδάλιον," are helpful.

*Wholly Blessed Apostles, the Sacred Ecumenical and Local Synods and the Individual Holy Fathers*) was published in Athens by the legal scholars G. Rhallēs and M. Potlēs from 1852 to 1859 in six volumes. It is the best of all available collections due to its strictly scientific and scholarly character. At the same time, it offers those interested in acquiring an understanding of Orthodox Canon Law the most complete account of its origin and development. Volume 1 contains the *Nomokanon in 14 Titles* with the commentary of Balsamōn. Volume 2 contains the *Apostolic Canons*, canons of the ecumenical councils and last two regional councils (*Prōtodeutera* in 861 and *Holy Wisdom* in 879/880), and the commentaries of Zōnaras, Balsamōn, and Aristēnos. Volume 3 contains canons of the remaining regional councils as in the preceding volume. Volume 4 contains canons of the Fathers, together with canons not ratified by an ecumenical council, yet having universal authority and recognition. Volume 5 contains canonical decrees of patriarchal synods from 911 to 1835, as well as imperial legislation from the time of Justinian to Andronikos (1226), among numerous other canonical sources. Volume 6 contains the *Syntagma* of Blastarēs.[43]

## 1.6 APPLICATION OF CANONS

Canons differ as to the object of their concern. There are canons that relate to faith and those that relate to ecclesiastical order and discipline. The former have as their purpose the preservation of revealed truth and, as such, are immutable. The latter regulate the external life of the faithful and can be changed to meet the needs of the Church whenever deemed necessary.[44] Such changes, however, must always be in keeping with the basic teachings of the government of the Church (Church polity) and with the Church's ethos and norms.

---

43 Mouratides, 101–104; see also Christophilopoulos, 1:36–37 and Milaš, 277–79.

44 For another approach, see Nicholas Afanasiev, "The Canons of the Church: Changeable or Unchangeable?" *St. Vladimir's Theological Quarterly* 11 (1967): 54–68; and the discussion of sources and methodology in the first part of the second volume of the present work.

In order for a canon to be applicable, the following conditions must be met: Internally, it must be adopted by the competent ecclesiastical authority; its content must be ecclesiastical; its essence must be in agreement with fundamental Church doctrines; and it must be intended for the benefit of the faithful. Externally, it must be officially promulgated so that its intended audience is aware of its existence, and the sanctions foreseen in the event of its violation must be upheld.

The Church's canons are binding for all her members. This is expressly stated in canon 2 of the Council in Trullo (the *Penthektē* Ecumenical Council): "No one is allowed to transgress or disregard the aforesaid canons."[45] The Fathers of the Seventh Ecumenical Council decreed the following in canon 1, relative to the preceding canon: "We (embrace) with gladness the divine canons, holding fast all the precepts of the same, complete and without change, whether they have been set forth by the holy trumpets of the Spirit, the renowned apostles, or by the six ecumenical councils, or by councils locally assembled for promulgating the decrees of the said ecumenical councils, or by our holy Fathers. For all these, being illumined by the same Spirit, defined such things as were expedient."[46]

From both these canons it is evident that the Fathers of both councils hold that all members of the Church, clergy and laity alike, are bound by the canons promulgated under their authority. Both canons make mention only of ecclesiastical legislation issued up to that time. However, this does not mean that the legislative work of the Church ended with the Seventh Ecumenical Council. This work is ongoing and will continue as long as the Church's mission in the world continues. Furthermore, this legislation is binding for all the Church's members as long as it follows the fundamental tenets of the Church.

The decrees of the Council in Trullo (*Penthektē* or *Quinisext Concilium*) and Seventh Ecumenical Councils in no way forbid change in the ecclesiastical legislation mentioned. Although canons touching on doctrine or morality are based on Holy Scripture and

---

45  Percival, 361.
46  Percival, 555.

are therefore absolute, it is expected that legislation regulating the external life of the Church will fluctuate with the Church's needs. When the need arises for change in the Church's legislation, only a council of equal or greater importance than that which introduced it has this authority. History has preserved examples of councils that either abrogated (abolished, annulled) or invested with new form the ecclesiastical legislation of previous councils. These examples serve as important precedents. Acceptable modifications must, however, retain the essence and spirit of the original legislation and harmonize with the fundamental tenets of the Church.[47]

Equally important to this principle is the authorization of a local church (understood as the self-governing church of a particular region) to maintain its own special rights. This privilege is asserted by Canon 39 of the Council in Trullo: "For the customs which obtain in each Church our divine Fathers also took pains should be maintained."[48] These rights regulate the external affairs of such a church and must conform to the spirit of the universal law of the Church in general.

## 1.7 ABROGATION OF CANONS

It has been established that canons containing a doctrinal truth are universal and unalterable. This is not the case with canons regulating the Church's outward life (relations with the state or with non-Orthodox Christians). These are canons of discipline and order. As such, they can be partially altered or totally changed if conditions call for it. A law can be abolished, amended, or refined by a body of the same authority as that which issued it, or by a superior authority. As the supreme legislative body in the Church, ecumenical councils have the authority to abolish ecclesiastical laws and replace them with others when reasons for doing so are justified.

A total change of a law or canon involves its abrogation and the loss of its validity. Such change can come about in one of two ways: by means of a formal decree, or by falling into disuse. For example,

---

47 See Appendix B: "Ecclesiastical Reform: At What Cost?"
48 Percival, 383.

canon 5 of the Holy Apostles states, "Let not a bishop, presbyter, or deacon put away his wife under pretense of religion; but if he put her away, let him be excommunicated; and if he persists, let him be deposed."[49] This was changed by decree in canon 12 of Trullo, which asserts, "Although it has been decreed that wives are not to be cast forth, nevertheless, that we may counsel for the better, we give command that no one ordained a bishop shall any longer live with his wife."[50]

Similarly, canons 37 of the Holy Apostles, 5 of 1 Nicea, and 19 of Chalcedon call for episcopal councils to be held in each province twice a year. These canons have been superseded by canons 8 of Trullo and 6 of 2 Nicea, which permit episcopal councils to be held once a year due to changed conditions in the Church. Canon 15 of Neocaesarea affirms, "Seven deacons according to the Acts of the Apostles should be appointed for each great city."[51] However, canon 16 of Trullo declares, "Whoever affirms that the number of deacons should be seven according to the saying of the Acts, should know that the reference in that passage is not to Deacons of the Mysteries but to such as serve tables."[52]

A law may also cease to be valid by falling into disuse ( ἀχρησία, desuetudo), or by the introduction of new legislation in its place. If the latter is the case, the disuse of the law must be justified, and any replacing legislation must be in harmony with the general spirit of the law according to canon 7 of Constantinople 861 (Prōtodeutera, or First-Second Council): "For nothing brought into existence illegally and disorderly can prejudice what has been canonically constituted."[53]

---

49  Percival, 594.
50  Percival, 370.
51  Percival, 86.
52  Percival, 373.
53  Rhallēs and Potlēs, 2:674.

A law may also cease to be valid when it was issued with limited intent,[54] or when it is no longer relevant,[55] or when it no longer corresponds to the contemporary needs of the Church. Because of entirely different circumstances, the Church may consider it necessary to abolish a law or adopt new laws to confront contemporary situations. In the latter case, the earlier laws are abolished according to a principle found in the legislative code *Basilika* of Emperor Leo VI: "Subsequent decrees prevail over those which preceded them."[56]

Partial change of a law abolishes, and sometimes replaces, part of the law. Whenever a new law appears, it is assumed, even if not expressly stated, that any content necessary was abolished to meet existing needs. As for still-applicable parts of the original law, they continue to apply unless otherwise noted.[57]

A law may also generally be in force while certain persons, whether legal (an institution) or natural, are exempted from it. Persons are exempted either through "privilege" (προνόμιον, *privilegium*) or "dispensation" (συγκατάβασις, *oikonomia, dispensatio*). In the first instance, privilege, a law may be in force for all but those for whom an exception is foreseen. In its place, another special law is applied for these persons. This special law is a privilege granted exclusively by the legislator, who under certain conditions can also abolish it. A privilege ceases when the cause for its existence disappears.[58]

---

54  See Trullo 3 in Percival, 362–63.

55  See, for example, Holy Apostles 84, which reflects a period in the early Church when she was governed separately from pagan society. As a result, action could be taken against her members who might be guilty of a political offence. When the Church was officially recognized by the state, such matters were then judged by the latter.

56  "Αἱ μεταγενεστέραι διατάξεις ἰσχυρότεραι τῶν πρὸ αὐτῶν εἰσιν," Book II, title 6, 5. See also Holy Apostles 5 as it relates to Trullo 12, and Holy Apostles 37, 1 Nicea 5, and Chalcedon 19 as they relate to Trullo 8 and 2 Nicea 6.

57  See Holy Wisdom 2, according to which a bishop embracing the monastic life must relinquish his episcopal office, whereas a hieromonk (ordained monastic) may still be elevated to the office of bishop.

58  For example, ecclesiastical property may be exempted from taxes only as long as it is under the possession of the Church.

A second instance of persons exempted from a law is dispensation. A dispensation is granted by the competent ecclesiastical authority and has a character of leniency and compassion for human frailty rather than urgency. This character is justified by the Church's desire to prevent any adverse consequences resulting from a strict observance of the law. The granting of an exception is based on the general welfare of all concerned. This premise exists in all legal systems; however, it finds its fullest expression in the Church's law, which is the law of grace. As such, it is characterized primarily by the spiritual attributes of compassion, understanding, and forgiveness.

As for the application of dispensation, the competent ecclesiastical authority granting it must follow strictly defined guidelines. Dispensation from a law of universal authority within the Church is prohibited. Dispensation from a law valid only locally is possible if spiritually justified.

The right to grant dispensation is the sole prerogative of the legislator (synod of bishops). This right can in turn be delegated to the legislator's subordinate authorities (individual bishops) within the limits prescribed by law and according to the express authorization of the superior legislative authority.[59] Furthermore, dispensation ceases upon termination of the original cause or if its request rested on false or pretentious grounds.

The institution of *oikonomia* as dispensation has been applied in the Church since the time of the apostles. Saint Paul's assertion "I have become all things to all men, that I might by all means save some,"[60] signifies a wide application of *oikonomia* throughout his

---

59  See Ancyra 2 in Percival, 63: "It is likewise decreed that deacons who have sacrificed and afterwards resumed the conflict, shall enjoy their other honors, but shall abstain from every sacred ministry, neither bringing forth the bread and the cup, nor making proclamations. Nevertheless, if any of the bishops shall observe in them distress of mind and meek humiliation, it shall be lawful to the bishops to grant more indulgence, or to take away what has been granted."

60  1 Cor 9:22.

ministry. The Fathers, too, often make use of it, especially with reference to penitential discipline. In his first letter to Amphilochios of Iconium, Saint Basil clearly recommends the use of *oikonomia* in dealing with the problem of certain heretics returning to the Church.[61]

*Oikonomia* has been exercised more in the Church of the East than of the West. A greater flexibility in applying the law is characteristic of the Eastern Church, as opposed to the strict application common in the Western Church.[62] In the Church of the West, the bishop of Rome alone has exclusive authority to dispense from strict adherence to the law. In the Church of the East, this authority is delegated to the bishop by his synod. In serious matters, it is always the synod that decides whether to exercise *oikonomia*. For important issues, the final and ultimate authority rests with an ecumenical council. As an ecclesiastical body of supreme administrative, legislative, and judiciary authority, it exercises *oikonomia* by its own right. Furthermore, it can alter or overrule the decision of any subordinate ecclesiastical authority.

---

61 See Basil 1; see also 1 Nicea 12, Trullo 102, and Gregory of Nyssa 4, 5, 8.

62 Examples that can be cited are the way the Western Church continues to forbid divorce under any condition, or the strict adherence to clerical celibacy in conformity to St. Paul's statements about marriage.

## II. ORGANIZATION AND POLITY OF THE CHURCH

The body of the Church is a mystery beyond rational comprehension, for it is an organization instituted by God and founded by our Lord Jesus Christ for the salvation and sanctification of humanity. Furthermore, it is an organization that is one and indivisible, human and divine, seen and unseen. According to the eminent canonist Nikodim Milaš: "The Church as a body, the head of which is Christ, is made up of all who are baptized, working for a common cause and striving for the realization of the purpose for which the Church was instituted. Because of this, the members of the Church are brothers and sisters, equal in the eyes of God, mutually sanctified and constituting a royal priesthood."[63] Therefore, the fundamental principle on which the organization of the Church rests is the union of human and divine into one body for a common purpose.

### 2.1 DISTINCTIONS OF MEMBERS OF THE CHURCH

The Church is composed of the clergy and the laity. In addition to these two orders is that of monks, who, in a sense, constitute an order between the clergy and the laity. The distinction between clergy and laity gives symbolic expression to the essence of the Church as a divine and human institution. The foundations for this distinction were laid by our Lord himself, who instituted a

---

63 Milaš, 299.

special order of the faithful for the exclusive stewardship of God's sacraments. This order is the clergy, which differs from the laity through the rite of ordination (χειροτονία).

Through the divinely instituted ceremony of ordination, divine grace descends through prayer and the laying on of hands by the bishop and confers on the candidate one of the three degrees of the priesthood. Those who belong to the highest degree of the priesthood constitute the hierarchy,[64] through which our Lord governs his Church. The divinely instituted hierarchy, the most important institution in the Church, defines and characterizes her structure as hierarchical. This structure signifies that it is not the will of the faithful that molds the visible Church, but the will of God, expressed by the hierarchy. To this end the hierarchy is called upon to apply with great care the Church's divine law, which expresses the will of God.[65]

## LAITY

The main distinction of the members of the Church into laity and clergy is not to be taken as a division or contrast among the faithful. Nor is it to be understood as a formation of privileged orders—in the sense of more rights and less obligations—or of varying degrees of importance. Through the sacrament of holy baptism, every believer partakes in the threefold office of our Lord—king, priest, and prophet. This participation does not afford the layperson the same character granted to the cleric through priesthood, yet all the faithful—clergy and laity alike—partake of the same Holy Spirit. Independent of race, descent, sex, social status, or age, all were raised to the status of children of God and have thereby acquired complete equality. Even the distinction into clergy and laity creates only external distinctions, in no way diminishing the basic equality of all the faithful and in no way introducing an essential discrepancy.[66]

---

64 This is the hierarchy of the Church in the narrow sense, limited only to the episcopacy.
65 Mouratides, 120.
66 Mouratides, 120–21.

The renowned canonist Hamilcar Alivizatos correctly observed the following regarding clergy and laity:

The clergy is the governing body in the Church; however, in spite of the prerogatives of honor and respect accorded to the clergy, the attribute of governing does not grant privileges which the laity does not have. As in the state, the members of a governing administration do not have more privileges than other citizens—the laity, too, is in no way inferior to the clergy. The obligation of the clergy to govern is at the same time an exclusive prerogative. The clergy has by divine law the obligation and the prerogative to govern the laity spiritually, just as the laity also by divine law has the obligation and the right to be governed by the clergy. To assure the success of his pastoral mission in the world, our Lord instituted the Apostles, and they the bishops, who together with the presbyters and deacons are obliged to govern the people of God—the laity—spiritually. The position held by both orders within the Church as the governing and the governed is justified when based upon rights and obligations simultaneously. The bishops together with the other clergy have not only the right but especially the obligation to govern the laity spiritually; on the other hand, the laity is not governed simply by obligation, but especially by right. The layperson has the right to be baptized, wed, buried, sanctified ecclesiastically, and the cleric has the obligation to perform all these ecclesiastical ceremonies as the instrument of the Church, who in no way does what he does on his own authority.[67]

Clergy and laity together are subject to the same law; therefore, they have the same basic obligations. Although the clergy's authority in the Church is relatively greater than that of the laity, the clergy is also accountable for more. The distinctions among the Church's members do not abolish the equality attained through baptism; on the contrary, their purpose is to strengthen the unity among them.

---

67  Quoted in Mouratides, 121–22.

The presence of the clergy facilitates the coordination of efforts to achieve the Church's mission on earth.

The active participation of the laity in ecclesiastical adminis-tration stresses the importance of this element for the formation of ecclesiastical life in general, without overlooking the special mission of the clergy. If the proper functioning of secular organiza-tions is dependent on their members' individual roles, this is much more the case when speaking about the Church, which is unlike any worldly organization.

The equality of the Church's members and their participation in the threefold office of our Lord results in the active involvement of the laity in the Church's government and general life. The only way the organization of the Church can function fully and effectively is through the unified cooperation of clergy and laity. The assistance of the laity in the administration of ecclesiastical matters ought to be met with the full cooperation and respect of the clergy. The formation and growth of the organization of the Church places on all her members the moral responsibility to work together for the realization of her lofty mission.

The significance of the entire body of the Church, clergy and laity, for the Church's organization is most evident in the acceptance of the common conscience (mind or φρόνημα of the Church)[68] of clergy and laity—ecclesiastical conscience—as the sovereign authority in the Orthodox Church. As this determines the ecumenicity of an ecumenical council, ecclesiastical conscience can be accurately called the highest authority in the Church.[69]

The participation of the laity in the formation of the life of the Church can be summarized in three ways: teaching authority (potestas magisterii), sanctifying authority (potestas ordinis), and administrative authority (potestas iurisdictionis). The basic exercise of teaching authority belongs to the clergy, although the laity can be authorized to contribute to the fuller expression of it. Contemporary examples of this are catechetical schoolteachers, lay theologians,

---

68  Fr. Georges Florovsky speaks of common conscience as "mind or phronema of the Church" in his essay "The Function of Tradition in the Ancient Church," in Bible, Church, Tradition: An Eastern Orthodox View (Belmont, MA: Nordland Publishing Co., 1972), 73–92.
69  Mouratides, 122–24.

and lay preachers. The role of the laity in sanctifying authority is more clearly passive. Nevertheless, there are situations when the laity is permitted to exercise this authority too: for example, the "baptism of necessity."[70] It is in administrative authority that the participation of the laity has always been greatest in the Orthodox Church. Contemporary examples include participation in parish councils, diocesan councils, and clergy-laity assemblies. In summary, only the common action of both clergy and laity along strictly defined lines is in keeping with the spirit of the Orthodox Church.[71]

## CLERGY

The clergy has existed from the time of the institution of the Church. As a body that exercises spiritual authority in the Church, its main missions are to spread and strengthen the Christian faith, perform sacred rites and acts, and govern the Church. Those who compose the clergy—clerics—are divided into major orders and minor orders. Major orders consist of bishops, presbyters, and deacons. The minor orders consist of sub-deacons, readers, and chanters. The early Church included other offices as well, such as exorcists and door keepers, now defunct.

The basis of the distinction between major and minor orders is the manner of institution. For major orders the manner of institution is the rite of ordination (χειροτονία), for minor orders, that of the laying on of hands and tonsure (χειροθεσία). The rite of ordination takes place within the sanctuary through invoking the grace of the Holy Spirit upon the candidate. The laying on of hands and tonsure by the bishop on the candidate for the minor orders takes place outside of the sanctuary. Doctrinally speaking, ordination is a sacrament, while the laying on of hands and tonsure

---

70 For more information on the "baptism of necessity" and baptism generally, see section 4.1.

71 See Milaš, 309, quoted in Mouratides, 125. On the role of the laity in the Orthodox Church, see J. Karmiris, *The Status and Ministry of the Laity in the Orthodox Church*, trans. E. Zachariades-Holmberg (Brookline, MA: Holy Cross Orthodox Press, 1994); see also Appendix B: "The Relationship between the Clergy and the People from a Canonical Perspective," and "Theological and Canonical Understandings."

is simply a holy ceremony. Through ordination one possesses the office of priesthood, gains entry into the hierarchy of the Church,[72] and participates in ecclesiastical authority.

Ecclesiastical authority is divided into sanctifying authority and governing authority. Sanctifying or teleturgical authority gives the clergy the right to perform the sacraments and other sacred acts, and magisterial authority grants clergy the right to preach the word of God. Governing authority, which includes legislative, administrative, and judiciary authorities, is the main authority of a legal nature. It is therefore the authority that most concerns the science of canon law.

Sanctifying authority differs from governing authority in several ways. Sanctifying authority is acquired through ordination. Governing authority is granted, and as such, it is a legal act. Sanctifying authority belongs only to the clergy, while governing authority is shared with the laity. The degree of sanctifying authority is increased through ordination from a lower to a higher degree of priesthood (deacon to presbyter, presbyter to bishop). Furthermore, it is forfeited if the penalty of defrocking[73] is inflicted, but it cannot be relinquished by resignation. Governing authority, however, is not permanent and may be relinquished by resignation.

As mentioned above, the clerical state is attained by ordination or the laying on of hands and tonsure. Ordination occurs in each degree of priesthood when it is raised from a lower degree. One may not be ordained in the same degree twice. The performance of ordination is the exclusive right of the bishop, which renders him the instrument through which authority is distributed in the Church. This right gives the office of bishop an exalted position within the organization of the Church. In order for the bishop to exercise this right, exact conditions (as defined by the canons) must be met. Failure to apply these conditions invalidates the ordination. The canonicity of the ordination depends on the presuppositions and qualifications of both the one ordaining and the ordinand.

---

72  This is the hierarchy of the Church in the broad sense, including all ranks of the clergy.

73  For more information on the extent and function of governing authority, see the section on governing authority under "Exclusive Rights of Provincial Bishops," in section 2.2, "Episcopal Polity."

## Qualifications of an Ordaining Hierarch

An ordaining bishop must have been canonically ordained and installed in his episcopal see, to which he must be personally and locally assigned. He must be in communion with the Orthodox Church whose priesthood stems from apostolic succession. He must not have been defrocked, nor be a schismatic or heretic. He must not have resigned but be active in his episcopal ministry, and he must not be self-ordained.

Depending on the situation of the ordaining bishop, the resulting ordination may be effective and canonical (ἰσχυρά) if he is in communion with the Orthodox Church, and if he is canonically ordained and installed. It may also be extraterritorial (παρ'ἐνορίαν) if he ordains outside his diocese. This defect can be lifted by the previous consent or subsequent approval of the locally competent bishop. For those ordained outside the Orthodox Church seeking communion with her, their ordination is considered ineffective and null (ἀνίσχυρος) if the ordaining bishop is in communion with an ecclesiastical body that does not recognize the sacrament of priesthood and apostolic succession or is self-ordained. Such an ordination cannot be subsequently recognized even by *oikonomia* since it is contrary to dogma.

With the permission of the local hierarch, an abbot who is a hieromonk may perform laying on of hands and tonsure on a reader or subdeacon for his monastery (2 Nicea 14 and Nikēphoros 6). The act of ordination ought to take place publicly in the church, preferably on a Sunday, Saturday, or feast day when as many people as possible can bear witness to the event. Canon 7 of Saint Theophilos requires that ordinations not be performed clandestinely.[74]

The ordination to each degree of the priesthood ought not to take place "at large" (ἀόριστος), but for a specific position within the organization of the Church. Canon 6 of Chalcedon strictly forbids at-large ordinations: "Neither presbyter, deacon, nor any of the ecclesiastical order shall be ordained at large, nor unless the person ordained is particularly appointed to a church in a city or village, or to a martyry, or to a monastery. And if any have

---

74  See Milaš, 381–82, quoted in Mouratides, 129.

been ordained without a charge, the Holy Synod decrees, to the reproach of the one ordaining, that such an ordination shall be inoperative, and that such shall nowhere be suffered to officiate."[75] An ordination by simony either through payment of money or with the intervention of secular authorities is unlawful and should not be recognized (Holy Apostles 29 and 30, Trullo 22, 2 Nicea 3 and 5, and Novel 6 of Justinian (535) chap. 1).

The validity of an ordination presupposes a lapse of time from one degree of ordination to the next (referred to as "interstices"). In addition, it assumes the free consent of the candidate, who must be unforced and mentally capable. Ordination to a higher degree, however, is compulsory. According to canon 31 of Carthage, the penalty for refusing to submit to ordination to a higher degree is the loss of the current degree.

### Qualifications of Candidates for Holy Orders[76]

The candidate must be a baptized, male Orthodox Christian. He must also have reached a level of maturity assuring the seriousness and responsibility expected of his priestly status. The first canonical decree setting the age of bishops at fifty is found in the *Apostolic Constitutions*.[77] Canon 14 of Trullo determines the age of thirty for a presbyter and twenty-five for a deacon. Canon 11 of Neocaesarea also determines the age of thirty for a presbyter.

In addition, a candidate must be of strong faith. Extreme care must be taken to prevent a candidate with shallow faith from entering the clergy. Related to this prerequisite is the prohibition against ordaining neophytes only recently baptized (Holy Apostles 80 and 1 Nicea 2, among others).[78] It is also prohibited to ordain

---

75 Percival, 271.

76 For an in-depth study of the qualifications of candidates for holy orders in the first five centuries and a theory of the canons and patristic texts about priesthood and the praxis of ministry, see Appendix B: *A Noble Task: Entry into the Clergy in the First Five Centuries.*

77 The *Apostolic Constitutions* appear among the anonymous codified works mentioned in section 1.2.

78 The impediment of recent conversion stems from uncertainty about the motivation for baptism, thereby questioning the candidate's stability of faith.

those who were baptized out of fear of imminent death. Canon 12 of Neocaesarea states that their faith stems not from conviction but from need.

Candidates must have the necessary theological preparation.[79] They must also be free from impediments such as bodily defects or mental disorders. Canon 79 of the Holy Apostles mentions deafness and blindness as impediments, not due to the defects themselves, but because they hinder a cleric from performing his liturgical functions. Any physical disabilities that might hinder ministerial tasks are barriers to ordination. Similarly, according to Canon 1 of 1 Nicea, castration is considered a hindrance to ordination, although only if this defect is self-inflicted,[80] not if it stems from birth or is the result of therapeutic treatment or barbaric persecution. Also, a candidate's marital status, married or celibate, must conform to what is required by the Church.[81]

Obstacles to ordination include: unlawful marriage[82] (Holy Apostles 19, Trullo 26), second marriage[83] (Holy Apostles 17, Trullo 3, Basil 12), marriage to a widow or divorcee, a non-virgin, or an adulteress—even if she and her lawful husband separate[84] (Holy Apostles 18), carnal sin with any person prior to marriage,[85] loss

---

79 Applied to the needs of the contemporary Church, this qualification requires candidates for ordination in the Greek Orthodox Archdiocese of America to be recipients of the Master of Divinity degree from an accredited Orthodox School of Theology.

80 The principle implied is that self-mutilation of any kind (e.g., vasectomy) renders one unfit for ordination.

81 Included in the candidate's canonical marital status is the expectation that his wife is of the Orthodox faith (Carthage 36).

82 Unlawful marriage is marriage with a person of a prohibited degree of relationship.

83 A second marriage is counted after baptism.

84 Mention is also made of a woman whose profession is socially unacceptable.

85 Neocaesarea 9 prohibits a priest who confesses a carnal sin spontaneously (αὐθορμήτως) following ordination from exercising sanctifying authority. A deacon is demoted to the rank of sub-deacon. Although this canon specifies a particular carnal sin, the principle allows for a broader application of all carnal sin. The issue of carnal sin must be assessed by the spiritual father together with the candidate for holy orders.

of good reputation[86] (Laodicea 12, 1 Nicea 9), and all offenses sanctioned by the canons.

An ordination performed in violation of these impediments is null and void (ἄκυρος) unless other provisions are made in the canons—as in the case of one who contracts an unlawful marriage in ignorance. In such a case, the candidate is suspended permanently rather than having his ordination annulled. An annulment is declared by the local bishop on behalf of his synod. Until the annulment is made publicly known, all sacred acts performed previously by a sanctioned priest are considered effective.[87]

## Consequences of Ordination

The priesthood imparts a permanent character. This means that should a defrocked priest be reinstated, he would not be re-ordained. The permanent character of the priesthood is considered a theological opinion (θεολογούμενον). This is in contrast to the Roman Catholic Church for which the permanent character of the priesthood is established dogma.

A cleric must not become involved in secular activity. He cannot contract a lawful marriage. Neither can he resign or voluntarily give up his priestly character. Furthermore, he must not swear an oath, but give an assurance on his priesthood. Finally, he has the right to be financially supported by the parish he serves.

## Loss of Priestly Authority

The status of priest cannot be given up by resignation; it can, however, be lost through deposition or defrocking. This is the most severe of all sanctions that can be imposed on a priest. Through deposition or defrocking, a priest is returned to the rank from which he came—either laity or monk. All sacraments performed by a defrocked priest are invalid/ineffective (ἀνίσχυρα).[88] A defrocked

---

86  The canons do not specify what precisely constitutes loss of good reputation; this is left to the discretion of the ordaining hierarch. Certainly, criminal acts condemned by civil law or canonical offenses mentioned by the canons constitute a loss of good reputation.

87  In this sense, the term "ἄκυρος" refers to an act, initially considered effective, which has been declared ineffective.

88  The term "ἀνίσχυρα" refers to acts that are ineffective by nature.

priest who defiantly performs sacraments is guilty of infringement and impersonating a priest (ἀντιποίησις). This is a severe offense calling for the penalty of major excommunication or anathema.

## Rights and Obligations of Clergy

Because of the special role of the clergy, especially in Orthodox lands, their legal status has traditionally differed from the laity according to the canons of the Church and laws of the state. While the clergy have ecclesiastical rights by divine right, they also have certain societal rights and privileges.

A basic right of the clerical status is its inviolate character. According to canon 3 of Constantinople (879), there were serious consequences attached to striking a bishop. There are also, by tradition and custom, various gestures of respect accorded the clergy. Historically, the clergy had the legal privilege and right to be tried by an ecclesiastical court (*privilegium fori*). Clerics involved in personal differences with others were tried by their ecclesiastical authorities and not in civil courts. Today this privilege is only of historical interest. Similarly, clerics ought not to take oaths in court, but to give assurance of the truth of their testimony upon their priesthood. Clerics have been also accorded exceptions in the fulfillment of certain political obligations, such as serving in the armed forces.[89]

Regardless of his degree of priesthood, the cleric must conform to certain obligations. His behavior in public must reflect the sacred character of the priesthood. As identified in the early sources, mention is made of intoxication, the frequenting of taverns and disreputable places, gambling, and usury (Holy Apostles 42, Trullo 50, Laodicea 24, Carthage 40).

In addition, the cleric must wear appropriate clothing reflecting his clerical office at all times (Trullo 27). He is prohibited from living with a *subintroducta*,[90] unless she is a close relative, i.e., mother or sister (Ancyra 19). He must not engage in any occupation unbecoming to the priesthood (e.g., running a tavern, leasing

---

89 Mouratides, 136–38.
90 A woman committed to virginity, while living with a man in spiritual marriage. The visible impropriety of such a relationship rendered it incompatible with the life of a cleric, hence an obstacle to priesthood in any form.

farmlands, or pursuing commerce). Although in some instances these occupations are perceived differently now, they nonetheless raise similar concerns about propriety for one engaged in ordained ministry. Consequently, great discretion should be used prior to involving oneself in extra-ecclesiastical activities for the purpose of profit (Trullo 9, 10; Carthage 16). To this list (and for the same reasons) should be added the exercise of a political office or involvement in secular affairs in general (Holy Apostles 81).[91]

## MONASTICS

Monks (or nuns) constitute a parallel body to both clergy and laity. This body first appeared as an organized ecclesiastical institution following a communal rule of life (κοινόβιον) at the beginning of the fourth century.

The status of a monk is acquired by monastic tonsure (μοναχικὴ κουρά, ἀπόκαρσις). In this religious ceremony, the hair of the candidate monk is cut crosswise, formally enlisting him in the ranks of the monastic brotherhood as a lawful and canonical member. During the ceremony of tonsure, the candidate monk takes monastic vows dedicating himself wholly to God. In them, he promises lifelong continence, poverty, and obedience until death to the commands of the abbot and brotherhood, under the condition that they are in harmony with the letter and spirit of Holy Scripture.

Entry into the status of a monk was considered an act of dedication from the very beginning of monasticism and took on a festive form. Its first expression consisted in abandoning one's worldly garments and putting on the monk's habit. By abandoning his worldly garments, the monk was considered dead to the things of the world. By putting on his monk's habit, he was beginning a new life of righteousness and sanctity.

Like the sacraments of baptism and priesthood, the ceremony of entry into the status of a monk is not repeated, unless its original performance was invalid.[92]

---

91  Mouratides, 138–39.
92  Mouratides, 139–45.

## 2.2 POLITY OF THE CHURCH

The term "polity" in canon law comes from secular law and refers to the institution or aggregate of institutions by which a state makes and implements the rules of action necessary to govern society. Because the organization of the Church is not regulated by the human element alone, the term "polity" as used in secular law does not perfectly correspond to the way it is understood in canon law. The polity of the Church is characterized by its dependence on both human and divine elements.

In any discussion of polity, the type of government (monarchy, republic, and so forth) is determined by its supreme power holder. In a monarchy, the source of supreme power is a king or emperor. This type of government is monarchical. In a democracy, the source of supreme power resides with the people, and the type of government is democratic. The supreme power holder in the government exercised by the Orthodox Church is an ecumenical synod. Her form of government therefore is synodal.

The ultimate source of all authority in the Church is the will of God as expressed by the hierarchy collectively in a synod. The Church's government is based on two main principles: her hierarchical organization, and the equality and active participation of all members of the Church—clergy and laity—in the formation of the Church's life.

These principles have existed in the Church since the time of the apostles. The unity and equality of all members of the Church were exemplified in the unity and equality among the apostles and their successors, the bishops. The active participation of the laity in Church government was also instituted by the apostles, who gave the laity the right to elect their own ecclesiastical ministers. The cooperation of all members of the Church in creating her life and laws is known as the principle of conciliarity and is the basis of Orthodox ecclesiology.[93]

The institution of the hierarchy by divine right assured the equal synodal representation of the entire one, holy, catholic, and apostolic Church. In this way, from a legal point of view, the

---

93 See Appendix B: *Primacy and Conciliarity*, 31; and "Lived Experience and Theoretical Differences," 190–92.

ecumenical synod constitutes the supreme collective body of government of the Church.

However, the decisions of this supreme body are subject to the rule of ecclesiastical conscience, which is the harmonious agreement of clergy and laity. The major importance given to ecclesiastical conscience (φρόνημα)[94] has safeguarded the democratic element found in the polity of the undivided Church.[95]

## ECUMENICAL SYNOD

The synodal government of the Orthodox Church is the government of the undivided Church and the essence of her spiritual organization, which transcends nature (ὑπερφυσική). Although made up of several self-governing local (autocephalous) churches, the Orthodox Church is a spiritual unity.

The unity of all autocephalous Orthodox churches is manifested in their common sacraments, doctrine, and principles of government. From an administrative viewpoint, they all enjoy the same independence; however, all recognize the ecumenical synod as the supreme legislative, administrative, and judiciary body of the Church. It is this common recognition that guarantees both their spiritual and legal unity.

An ecumenical synod is an assembly of bishops with active positions in the Church, which gathers—if possible from all parts of the Christian world—for the purpose of common deliberation and decision on ecclesiastical issues which concern the universal Church. In order for a synod to be considered ecumenical, it must fulfill certain external and internal conditions.

With regard to external conditions, all local churches must be in attendance. If all bishops with active positions cannot attend in person, they should at least be represented or make known their intentions by letter. The number of participating bishops is not

---

94   See the discussion of laity under Chapter II, "Organization and Polity of the Church."

95   Mouratides, 148–52. See also Ἀμίλκας Ἀλιβιζάτος, "Ἡ Συνείδησις τῆς Ἐκκλησίας" [The Conscience of the Church], Ἐπιστημονικὴ ἐπετηρὶς τῆς Θεολογικῆς Σχολῆς τοῦ Πανεπιστημίου Ἀθηνῶν 10 (1954).

a determining factor of a synod's ecumenicity. History preserves examples of local councils in which more Fathers participated than in some ecumenical synods. Nevertheless, they still retained their local character. The Second Ecumenical Council of Constantinople in 381 had between 150 or 180 Fathers in attendance, while the Local Council of Carthage in 419 had over 300 Fathers. Equally important is the fact that decisions of an ecumenical council must be accepted by all local churches and by clergy and laity alike, which is evidence of ecclesiastical conscience about the issues discussed.[96]

As for internal conditions, issues discussed at an ecumenical synod must pertain to the Church Universal. Doctrine or organization and government of the Church Universal are examples of such issues. Furthermore, decisions must express what was always believed by all, everywhere. Fulfilling these conditions, both external and internal, constitutes a fundamental doctrine of the Orthodox Church.[97]

Matters for which an ecumenical council is competent include defining dogma, determining authentic ecclesiastical tradition, reviewing canons of all previous councils, designating all aspects of ecclesiastical administration, defining the ranks and privileges of the hierarchy, constituting a court of highest instance, and promulgating decrees for the Church Universal.

An ecumenical council is convened for matters of utmost importance, especially dogmatic issues. Matters of secondary importance can be resolved by a pan-Orthodox council, a synaxis of primates, or an exchange of letters, having the force of official decisions of the local churches. These means of resolving matters of secondary importance can be applied as temporary solutions pending their final approval by a future ecumenical council.[98]

---

96 See Ἀμίλκας Ἀλιβιζάτος, "Ἡ Συνείδησις τῆς Ἐκκλησίας" [The Conscience of the Church], 33ff., quoted in Mouratides, 172.

97 Mouratides, 172–73.

98 Mouratides, 173–74. See also Appendix B: "The Synodal Structure of the Orthodox Church," 71–75.

## Episcopal Polity

### Candidates to the Episcopacy

Because the episcopal office is the highest-ranking office in the structure of the Church, the holy canons require certain special qualifications for bishops beyond what is usually required of the priesthood, irrespective of degree. First and foremost, the bishop must be fully mature. While the office of deacon might be granted to a candidate not fully mature, in anticipation of his maturity after some experience, the office of bishop does not make such an allowance. Originally, the age of fifty was determined for a bishop. However, it was eventually lowered to the considerably younger age of thirty, providing the candidate showed signs of maturity.

Candidates for bishop must also possess deep faith and live a virtuous, irreproachable life tested over many years (Laodicea 12). These are requirements examined by the holy synod upon reviewing a candidate's qualifications prior to approval. Equally important are the bishop's knowledge of Scripture and the canons of the Church (2 Nicea 2).

A candidate who is not a monk must accept monastic tonsure and be celibate. He must not, however, take major vows (*great schēma*). Those who take major vows are bound to absolute obedience, a rule incompatible with the status of a bishop, who must be held accountable only to his synod.[99]

### Election, Ordination, and Affirmation of Bishops

Two methods for the election and consecration of bishops are employed in the Orthodox Church. Bishops may be elected by the competent episcopal synod and ratified by the secular authority (where church-state relations require such ratification). Within the Ecumenical Patriarchate of Constantinople, the holy synod draws up a list of candidates with the necessary requirements. From these candidates, three are chosen who are considered the most qualified (τριπρόσωπον). Of the three, the holy synod elects one as bishop. Bishops may also be elected by an assembly, in which the

---

99 Milaš, 495–98.

hierarchy and representatives from among the laity participate. This is the case with the Church of Cyprus.[100]

The act of publicly announcing the ratification of an episcopal candidate's election and the appointment by his ecclesiastical authority (the synod) is called an "affirmation" (μήνυμα). This act usually takes place within a church on the day before the episcopal ordination. At this time, the candidate officially and publicly accepts his election to the office of bishop. On the day of his episcopal ordination, and in the presence of all the clergy and the laity, the candidate recites the creed and makes a solemn affirmation of acceptance. He affirms that he will uphold the holy tradition of the Church, that he accepts all of the teachings of the Church, that he will maintain the canons of the Church, and that he will obey his superior ecclesiastical authority. He affirms that he will exercise his authority according to conscience, that he will fill all necessary posts in the administration of the Church, and that he will make the expected pastoral visitations throughout his diocese. He affirms that he has not committed simony to attain his office, that he has done nothing contrary to the holy canons, and that he will not become involved in secular affairs. Finally, he vows that he makes this affirmation in full consciousness of the consequences of his disavowal. The newly ordained bishop then receives from his ecclesiastical superior the "document of authorization" (ἔνταλμα/ ἐνταλτήριον), which lists the guidelines and instructions pertaining to his episcopal ministry.[101]

## Consequences of Episcopal Ordination

A bishop must be ordained for a particular see (Holy Apostles 14, 1 Nicea 15). Once ordained for a particular see, a bishop ordinarily cannot abandon it. If, for reasons beyond his control, a bishop does not have access to his see (e.g., the clergy and the laity dispute his election), he nevertheless still retains the privileges of his office.

---

100 See Milaš, 499–514, for a detailed overview of the election of bishops throughout the Church's history. For an account of the current process related to the election of bishops in the Greek Orthodox Archdiocese of America, see *Charter of the Greek Orthodox Archdiocese of America*, 2003, Articles 13–15, pp. 9–10, http://www.goarch.org/archdiocese/documents (accessed on July 11, 2022).
101 Milaš, 515–16.

He can still ordain clerics for his see and administer its affairs from outside its boundaries. Although an episcopal synod has the authority to sanction a bishop's transfer, such a transaction is rare. In his own see, a bishop is independent *ipso jure* (by his own right). The authority exercised by the bishop in his own diocese is exclusive, seen as a marital relationship of the bishop to his diocese; therefore, coexistence of more than one bishop within the same diocese is not permitted (1 Nicea 8). Finally, a bishop may not be reduced to the rank of presbyter (Chalcedon 29).[102]

## Mutual Relations of Bishops

All bishops are equal with regard to priestly authority. There are different degrees of administrative authority, however, and this regulates the relations of bishops among themselves. With regard to the relationship between a bishop and his superior ecclesiastical authority, he must fulfill the directives of the synod, report all diocesan matters of importance, participate in the synod when invited, refrain from transactions outside his jurisdiction without the synod's prior approval, and commemorate the name of his superior ecclesiastical authority. Bishops of equal rank also have obligations to one another. A bishop must honor a spiritual court's decisions regarding clergy or laity from another jurisdiction, must not accept in his jurisdiction any cleric or layman without the necessary letters of introduction (for a cleric or layman) or release (for clerics), and must concede a surplus number of clerics to jurisdictions where they are lacking.[103]

## Exclusive Rights of Provincial Bishops

### Teaching Authority

The office of the bishop reflects the three offices of Christ, who is prophet, priest, and king (teaching, sanctifying, and governing offices). As teacher, the bishop is the source of teaching authority in his administrative jurisdiction. As such, he has the right and obligation both to spread the faith and to see that it is kept inviolate. This is accomplished through his authority to teach, sanctify, and

---

102 Milaš, 517–20.
103 Milaš, 520–22.

administer within his diocese. Teaching authority is especially manifested in preaching. It is on the bishop's authority that the clergy under him are permitted to preach. Qualified laymen, too, may preach with the bishop's blessing. The bishop is responsible for supervising the training of the clergy and the teaching of religion in general. This is accomplished through his efforts to preserve the purity of the faith and to instruct the clergy and laity in matters of social and moral concern.[104]

### Sanctifying Authority

As chief priest (ἀρχιερεύς), the bishop has certain rights emanating from his sanctifying authority. He ordains all clerics in his jurisdiction, in both major and minor orders. He may also ordain clerics for another jurisdiction upon the request of a candidate's authorized bishop. He promotes all clerics in the adminirative hierarchy (archdeacon, protopresbyter, chancellor, archimandrite, etc.). He consecrates the holy *myron* (Carthage 6), churches, and *antimēnsia* (plural, ἀντιμήνσια; singular, ἀντιμήνσιον), the consecrated cloth on which the Divine Liturgy is celebrated (Carthage 6). He remits sins through the sacrament of penance and conveys this authority to father confessors through the ἐνταλτήριον γράμμα, the document authorizing a presbyter to hear confessions and grant remission of sins. He consecrates nuns. As for monks, an abbot has the right to perform the monastic tonsure of monks under his authority without the bishop's previous consent. The bishop also grants permission for all religious ceremonies, including litanies, within his jurisdiction.[105]

### Governing Authority[106]

As chief shepherd (ἀρχιποιμήν) reflecting the office of king, the bishop exercises governing authority within his diocese. Governing authority encompasses aspects of legislative, judiciary, and administrative authorities.

The legal basis for the bishop's legislative authority lies in his independent status within his jurisdiction. He is invested with the

---

104 Milaš, 522–26.
105 Milaš, 526–28.
106 Governing authority in the broad sense includes legislative, judiciary, and administrative (namely, supervision and management) authorities.

absolute right to regulate the affairs of his jurisdiction for both clergy and laity. The bishop's legislative authority fills omissions in the legislation laid down by the holy canons. These omissions are partly due to the fact that our law is not preventive law, which anticipates a problem before it arises, but corrective law, which treats a problem once it has occurred. The canons also do not cover all possible problems that might arise. Consequently, the local bishops are invested with the authority to resolve these issues. Any legislative measures enacted by the bishop under this authority must be in harmony with the spirit of the holy canons. These legislative measures become effective through pastoral epistles issued by the bishop to his flock. Pastoral epistles containing legislative decrees must also provide justification for them. These epistles may concern only the laity, in which case they must be read publicly in church by the parish clergy. Epistles concerning only the clergy are called encyclical epistles.[107]

The bishop's right to grant *oikonomia* is accorded only to the legislator. According to this premise, the bishop has the absolute right to grant an exception from any decrees that he has issued based on his individual legislative authority. He has only a relative right, however, to do so from all other legislation. Exceptions to legislation promulgated for the universal Church may only be granted by an ecumenical council, and not by any individual bishop.[108] Neither may a bishop grant *oikonomia* for legislation promulgated by the synod of an autocephalous church. This right can be exercised only by the synod itself. The bishop does have the right to release individuals, by exception, from a strict adherence to the law, depending on circumstances and its effect on the Church.

Out of pastoral consideration, the bishop has the right to grant *oikonomia* in several matters not specifically addressed in legislative texts but upheld by long-standing canonical tradition. In matters of marriage, he may allow an exception when there is a physical or

---

107 Milaš, 528, 646–49.

108 This should not be confused by a holy synod of a local church applying canons, either through strictness or *oikonomia*, through its own administrative authority as long as the canonicity of its decisions are received by the other local churches. Such administration of the canons must be distinguished from changing the text itself of a canon.

spiritual impediment to the prospective marital relationship, if it is not of a forbidden degree. If conditions warrant, he may permit the celebration of holy matrimony on feast days and during periods of the ecclesiastical year (e.g., Lent) when it would otherwise be prohibited. He may release a person from vows, with exception of monastic vows. He may exercise leniency in matters pertaining to the prerequisites of ordination (e.g., age or theological training), providing that it serves the best interests of the Church. He may also permit the consumption of prohibited foods for medical reasons during periods of fasting, and permit work due to financial need on feast days.[109]

The bishop's judiciary authority is exercised in the infliction of ecclesiastical penalties on all clerics and laypersons within his administrative jurisdiction who are guilty of an ecclesiastical offense.[110]

Administrative authority[111] is the broadest sphere of authority exercised by the bishop. Included within its scope is the bishop's selection of the worthiest candidates for ordination. In addition to selecting candidates, he assumes responsibility for their training and formation, defines the extent of their ministry, and closely supervises their achievements. Furthermore, all monasteries, parochial schools, and ecclesiastical institutions within his diocese are under his authority. He also oversees all legacies and bequests to the church.

The bishop attains firsthand knowledge of parochial affairs by pastoral visitations. During these visitations, he may examine whether all ecclesiastical functions are performed at the proper time, the conduct of the clergy, the maintenance of records and documents, the administration of ecclesiastical property, and the organization of religious education and pastoral outreach programs.[112]

---

109 Milaš, 528–30.
110 Regarding the exercise of judiciary authority in reaching decisions of ecclesiastical discipline, see section 3.1, "Ecclesiastical Penitential Law."
111 Administrative authority in the narrow sense of supervision and management.
112 Milaš, 530–34.

Under certain circumstances, a bishop can be released from his see and the administrative authority connected with it while retaining his priesthood. These circumstances include the sentence of lifelong suspension (ἀργία), deposition from his episcopal throne, monastic tonsure (great schēma), or resignation for reasons of health or old age.

## Auxiliary Bishops and
## Rural Bishops, Chōrepiskopoi (Χωρεπίσκοποι)

The office of auxiliary bishop was preceded in the early Church by the office of rural bishop, chōrepiskopos (χωρεπίσκοπος). The institution of chōrepiskopoi dates to the third century, when they were assigned by the bishop of an urban see to administer the affairs of its outlying regions. Even though the chōrepiskopoi had received episcopal ordination, they did not exercise episcopal authority independently in the region for which they were responsible. In this sense, their status was anomalous. However, it was not considered an at-large ordination (ἀπολελυμένη χειροτονία) either, since they were responsible for administering a designated region. The chōrepiskopoi differ from auxiliary bishops because chōrepiskopoi were attached to the rural area that they administered in the name of the bishop of the urban see. Auxiliary bishops—although bearing the title of a once-active episcopal see where they have no authority—are not permanently attached to any particular see, but exercise their office wherever needed, under their ecclesiastical superior (archbishop or metropolitan).[113]

## Presbyters

Next in rank to the bishop is the presbyter. The presbyter receives his appointment from the bishop, who ordains him and assigns him to a parish. The presbyter, or parish priest, is the direct representative of the bishop in the parish.

Within his parish, the parish priest has full responsibility. However, the administration of parish affairs is carried out in the name of the bishop from whom he received his priestly authority. The priest also exercises this authority through the sermons

---

113 Milaš, 546–47.

he preaches, the ceremonial functions he performs, and the administration he exercises within the jurisdiction of his bishop. None of these prerogatives can be exercised in another jurisdiction without the authorization (ἔνταλμα/ἐνταλτήριον) of the local bishop. Authorization is granted based on a letter of introduction or release, the documentary evidence by which a bishop authorizes a cleric within his jurisdiction to exercise priestly authority. The presbyter's parish is a subsection of an organically united greater diocese. Consequently, the parish is totally dependent on its assigned bishop. However, once the presbyter is appointed and installed in his parish, he exercises his rights and obligations freely, using the priestly authority he was endowed with at ordination.

Furthermore, the bishop cannot suspend or revoke the presbyter's authority at random, but only on extremely serious grounds and following an ecclesiastical court decision. Even then, the suspension is temporary until the case is reviewed and decided on definitively. Only an ecclesiastical court ruling can suspend the exercise of priestly authority permanently. Although this authority is transferred through the bishop, it emanates from the apostles collectively. It can therefore only be definitively suspended by a collective organ such as an ecclesiastical court.[114]

## APPOINTMENT OF PARISH CLERGY

The following is a general canonical overview of the relationship between bishops, parish clergy, and parish councils. Within the canonical tradition of the Orthodox Church, hierarchs possess the sole authority to appoint and remove any clergy to and from parishes. For example, the bishop would act as sole judge for acceptance or rejection of any petition by a parish council for dismissal or removal of clergy within his jurisdiction. All parish clergy are subject to the direct supervision of their bishop and not subject to any local rules and regulations of the parish. In the canonical tradition of the Church, the bishop approves all membership of a parish council in a parish under his jurisdiction, whose purpose is administrative in function.

---

114 Milaš, 575–77.

Consistent with the canonical tradition of the Church, the parish council provides for the priest's livelihood in accordance with standards that are reviewed and approved by his hierarch. When transferred, reassigned, or removed, a priest of a parish is answerable to his hierarch for an accounting of all church property used for sacred worship and required specifically to account for parish records. These requirements are in accordance with the canon law of the Orthodox Church. The following are the texts of Holy Apostles canons 38 and 41:

Holy Apostles canon 38 - Let the Bishop have the care of all ecclesiastical matters [things/goods of the Church] and let him manage them, on the understanding that God is overseeing and supervising. Let him not be allowed to appropriate anything therefrom or to give God's things to his relatives. If they be indigent, let him provide for them as indigents, but let him not trade off things of the Church under this pretext.[115]

Holy Apostles canon 41 – We command that the bishop have authority over the property of the Church. For if the precious souls of human beings ought to be entrusted to him, there is little need of any special injunction concerning money; so that everything may be entrusted to be governed in accordance with his authority, and he may grant to those in need through the presbyters and deacons with the fear of God and all reverence, while he himself may partake thereof whatever he needs (if he needs anything) for his necessary wants, and for brethren who are his guests, so as not to deprive them of anything, in any manner. For God's law has enjoined that those who serve at the altar are to be maintained at the altar's expense. The more so in view of the fact that not even a soldier ever bears arms against belligerents at his own expense.[116]

115 Rhallēs and Potlēs, 2:52.
116 Rhallēs and Potlēs, 2:57.

## III. ADMINISTRATION OF THE CHURCH

The administration of the Church encompasses the different ways the hierarchy exercises authority and the faithful experience it. This authority falls into three categories: teaching authority, sanctifying authority, and governing authority.

Teaching authority includes preaching, maintaining catechetical schools for teaching the faith, and promoting the faith through the publication of books and articles.

Sanctifying authority is exercised in the celebration of the sacraments. The presbyter is invested with the authority to perform all sacraments except ordination (reserved exclusively to the episcopacy).

Governing authority in the Church is a broad category and encompasses several different aspects. In the full sense of the term, it includes legislative authority (the right to promulgate legislation), judiciary authority (the right to defend justice), and administrative authority (the right to supervise and manage the Church's interests).[117] While this work cannot cover all the laws that deal with Church administration, representative examples of some aspects of governing authority follow.[118]

---

117 Governing authority is exercised in all local churches. For an assessment of the challenges local churches (jurisdictions) face in America, see Appendix B: "Diaspora vs. Local Church/Churches: The Specific Problems of America"; see also "The Harmonization of Canonical Order."

118 See also Chapter V: "Governance of the Local Church."

## 3.1 ECCLESIASTICAL PENITENTIAL LAW

Penitential law, which falls under judiciary authority, exists to facilitate the exercise of justice as foreseen in the canons. Its ultimate purpose is not, except in rare circumstances, to seek punishment of the transgressor, but to restore the transgressor to communion with the Church through repentance. Ecclesiastical penitential law concerns the various kinds of ecclesiastical sanctions imposed according to ecclesiastical practice. The following material deals both with sanctions imposed and the various ecclesiastical offenses committed to incur such sanctions.[119]

### ECCLESIASTICAL SANCTIONS

Ecclesiastical sanctions are divided into four categories according to whom they affect. Certain sanctions may be imposed on all members of the Church, clerics alone, both clerics and monks, or on monks alone.

### Sanctions Imposed upon All Members of the Church

According to the authority granted by our Lord to the apostles, and through them to their successors the bishops, bishops are those who exercise judiciary authority in the Church.[120] The sacrament of penance is one way judiciary authority is exercised. In this sacrament, acts of penance (ἐπιτίμια) may be prescribed for all members of the Church. The most commonly prescribed act of penance recommended by the canons is minor excommunication, which is temporary exclusion from the holy Eucharist.[121] The exercise of judiciary authority through the sacrament of penance

---

119 A characteristic component in the exercise of penitential discipline in the Orthodox Church is the spirit of compassion. To better understand the concept of compassion within the context of penitential discipline, see Appendix B: "The Spirit of Compassion in the Canonical Tradition of the Church."

120 Matt 18:18: "Whatever you bind on earth will be bound in heaven, and whatever you loose on earth will be loosed in heaven."

121 Other acts of penance are frequent prayer, rigid fasting, charity, reading religious books, and making pilgrimages.

can be carried out by the bishop personally or by a duly authorized priest. This authority is issued through a letter of authorization (ἐνταλτήριον γράμμα). Nevertheless, in such instances, it is necessary that such decisions of authorized priests be endorsed by their bishops. Canonically, both the bishop and his authorized priests exercise judiciary authority through penance only within the boundaries of their administrative jurisdiction.

Canonical decrees define how the sacrament of penance is administered. Accordingly, father confessors are not permitted to hear the confessions of those belonging to another faith. Also, confession is to be administered individually and is to be kept strictly secret.[122] Violation of this secrecy is subject to severe sanctions. Traditional piety calls for confession to be practiced at least once a year after one's seventh year of age. Acts of penance imposed are not punitive in character, but therapeutic. The manner in which penance is imposed is subject to the discretion of the father confessor.[123] If appealed to by the penitent, the bishop has the authority to mitigate or increase its severity.

If exclusion from Holy Communion is imposed by a father confessor, no other confessor—under ordinary circumstances—has the right to lessen the prescribed period of exclusion. Exceptions include the death of the original father confessor or the imminent death of the penitent.[124] In the latter instance, any priest can give the absolution.[125]

The most severe of all ecclesiastical sanctions is anathema or major excommunication. It consists of the total and absolute

---

122 Saint Nikēphoros 27, 28; Saint Basil 34.
123 Trullo 102 is the definitive canon that provides the criteria for applying *oikonomia* in the sacrament of penance.
124 Carthage 7.
125 Under normal circumstances, the priest should consult with the bishop before giving absolution or communing someone formally excluded.

expulsion of the sentenced person from the communion of the Church. The practice of anathema, based on Holy Scripture, can be found throughout the history of the Church.[126] Because of its severity, it is rarely applied, and usually only as a last resort in the hope that the person anathematized will seek forgiveness through repentance. The ecclesiastical sanction of anathema can also be imposed posthumously, as well as having its consequences extend beyond death. Anathema can also be lifted after death.[127]

Another sanction that may be imposed on all members of the Church is the forfeiture of an ecclesiastical burial. This is the only sanction in our penitential law imposed automatically once the offense has been committed, without a spiritual court decision. Persons deprived of an ecclesiastical burial are those on whom anathema has been inflicted without being repealed, those who died as a result of a duel, those who died from suicide unrepentant (unless it can be proven that suicide was the result of a mental disorder), those who married outside the Orthodox Church, and those who have been cremated.

## Sanctions Imposed upon Clerics

Ecclesiastical sanctions imposed only on clerics are defrocking/deposition, degradation/demotion, suspension, monetary fines, and, for bishops, loss of seniority or forfeiture of episcopal throne. Defrocking or deposition (καθαίρεσις) removes all priestly authority from a cleric and returns him to his previous order, either that of

---

126 In contrast to assigned penance, anathema is not a temporary exclusion from communion and is not conditioned by a time limitation. Scriptural support of anathema is to be found in the following passages: Matt 12:31–32, where mention is made of the unpardonable sin of ascribing to Satan the works of the Holy Spirit, cf. Mark 3:28–30; see also Matt 18:15–18, regarding discipline and forgiveness in the Church: "Let him be to you like a heathen and a tax collector"; Acts 8:9–24, concerning the case of Simon the sorcerer; 1 Cor 5:1–5, where immorality is rebuked and discipline commanded: "Deliver such a one to Satan for the destruction of the flesh, that his spirit may be saved in the day of the Lord Jesus", cf. vv. 9–13; see also 1 Tim 1:19–20, 2 Tim 3:1–5, Titus 3:10–11, and note 2 Cor 2:5–11, where mention of forgiveness is made following repentance.

127 Anathema imposed posthumously on a teacher of heresy, for example, serves to protect those who might otherwise fall victim to false teaching. A related consequence is the prohibition of public prayer for those anathematized.

layperson or monk. Sacraments performed by a defrocked cleric are invalid (ἀνίσχυρα).[128]

Degradation or demotion (ὑποβιβασμός) demotes a cleric to a lower degree in the clergy.[129] Defrocking and degradation are different in that a defrocked cleric is deprived of both priestly authority and administrative authority, whereas a degraded cleric is deprived only of administrative authority. A cleric may also be temporarily prevented from exercising both priestly and administrative authority by suspension (ἀργία). Sacraments performed by a suspended cleric are not invalid; however, their performance in violation of the suspension may lead to stricter sanctions. Clerics may also have monetary fines imposed on them as a sanction for specific acts of wrongdoing, as determined by an ecclesiastical court.[130]

Certain sanctions pertain only to bishops: loss of seniority within the hierarchy and forfeiture of episcopal throne. When a bishop is sanctioned with forfeiture of his episcopal throne, he nevertheless retains his episcopal rank. He may therefore perform all the sacraments corresponding to it, providing he has the approval of the local bishop.[131]

---

128 This is due to the fact that they are devoid of divine grace.

129 According to Chalcedon 4, degradation of a bishop to the rank of presbyter is disapproved of in principle. Once, however, in Trullo 20, a bishop who is discovered publicly teaching in a city under another hierarch's jurisdiction without permission is described as subject to the following sanction: "Let him cease from the episcopate but let him exercise the functions of the presbyterate." See Christophilopoulos, 3:34–35.

130 It should be noted that each bishop has the competence within the borders of his eparchy to impose sanctions on clergy who fall into ecclesiastical offenses of less significance, such as a written reprimand, temporary suspension, and forfeiture of rank (ecclesiastical *offikion* of Archimandrite, Protopresbyter, and so forth). For example, in the case of the Greek Orthodox Archdiocese of America, see Protocol 304, *Regulations of Spiritual Courts of the Holy Archdiocese of America*, March 20, 2014, article 1, § 2.

131 A basic principle of our canonical tradition requires approval of the bishop in whose administrative jurisdiction any sacrament is performed.

## Sanctions Imposed upon Clerics and Monastics

Sanctions imposed on both clerics and monastics include transfer from assignment, removal from administrative office (for example, chancellor of metropolis, abbot of monastery, and so forth), corporal confinement (usually within a monastery), and censure (called ἐπίπληξις when imposed upon priests and monastics and μομφή when imposed upon bishops).

## Sanctions Imposed upon Monastics

Finally, some sanctions are imposed only on monastics. These include expulsion from the monastery, denial of daily ration, and enhanced prayer.

### ECCLESIASTICAL OFFENSES

Ecclesiastical offenses are too numerous to list in their totality here. Some of the most egregious offenses, however, deserve special attention. Apostasy, heresy, and schism all involve the denial of some aspect of faith or authority. Apostasy is the denial of the Christian faith entirely and acceptance of another, or no faith at all. Heresy is the denial of, or deviation from, a fundamental doctrine of the Orthodox Church. Both of these offenses call for the most severe of sanctions, anathema, in the hope that persons so sanctioned will seek repentance and that the community will be protected from their influence.[132] Schism involves denial of obedience to the canonical ecclesiastical authority through the formation of an independent religious community.

Simony, another serious ecclesiastical offense, is the trading of divine grace in commerce. This usually involves the receipt or promise of payment in return for the exercise of ecclesiastical privileges. Named after Simon in the book of Acts for his attempt to purchase the power of the Holy Spirit,[133] simony has been seen as the first heresy of the Church. It is also characterized by deceit,

---

132 One guilty of apostasy is usually sanctioned with anathema, especially if the apostate poses a threat to the purity of the faith. In contrast to an apostate, the heretic still retains the Christian faith, but may pose the same threat to the purity of the faith. Therefore, both may be confronted with anathema.
133 Acts 8:9–24.

as it typically involves tempting others to believe that they may buy grace.

Sacrilege (ἱεροσυλία) involves the removal or theft of consecrated ecclesiastical property (moveable or immoveable).[134] An object removed or stolen need not be taken from a place of worship, but from anywhere it may be stored. Sacrilege also includes the act of reclaiming an object by one who has dedicated it to the Church.

Other examples of serious ecclesiastical offenses are the violation of graves (τυμβωρυχία); perjury (ψευδορκία) or telling a lie under oath; and performing sacraments extraterritorially (παρ'ἐνορίαν δράσις), or without the authorization of the bishop in whose administrative jurisdiction they take place. Betrayal of the secrecy of holy confession, neglect of ecclesiastical rubrics in the Typikon (Τυπικόν), or neglect of general pastoral obligations are also major ecclesiastical offenses and prompt severe sanctions for the guilty party.[135]

## ECCLESIASTICAL PENITENTIAL LAW OF PROCEDURE

Ecclesiastical judiciary authority originates from the Church's place in society as an independent and self-governing institution. The Church exercises this authority by divine right when her interests are challenged or violated. It is then that she invokes all the means at her disposal against those who would disturb established order, thereby preventing the free exercise of her mission.

The foundation of this authority was established by our Lord himself when he addressed his disciples in Matt 18:15–17: "If your brother sins against you, go and tell him his fault between you and him alone. If he hears you, you have gained your brother. But if he will not hear, take with you one or two more, that 'by the mouth of two or three witnesses every word may be established.' And if he refuses to hear them, tell it to the church. But if he refuses even to hear the church, let him be to you like a heathen and a tax collector."

---

134 Arbitrary removal from a church of unconsecrated items, such as ecclesiastical furniture, does not constitute an act of sacrilege, but theft.

135 Regarding the pastoral dimension of penitential discipline, see Appendix B: "The Interface of Pastoral Ministry and the Holy Canons," 185–92. See also Appendix B: "Lived Experience and Theoretical Differences," 192–96.

The holy canons speak of the bishop as the figure who embodies judiciary authority over members of the Church.[136] Presbyters can exercise judiciary authority only when authorized by their bishop. In such an instance, however, the ultimate decision rests with the bishop alone. Ecclesiastical courts judge all cases related to improper conduct of the clergy or violations in their performance of sacred acts. With regard to the laity, ecclesiastical courts adjudicate matters related to improper conduct, but also those of marriage and divorce, as well as canonical issues related to the Orthodox faith.

## ECCLESIASTICAL COURTS[137]

Judiciary authority, like all other authority in the Church, is canonically exercised collectively by a synod. Nevertheless, clerical offenses that do not cause scandal and can be treated individually through admonition and censure are subject to the bishop's personal judiciary authority.[138] Penalties are only corrective measures and can be suspended if the penalized individual repents.

An episcopal court is convened if offenses are of a serious nature. It is constituted by the local bishop (the presiding hierarch) and clerics (presbyters) selected by him. It is a court of first instance. Decisions are reached only by the hierarch since the role of participating clerics is mainly advisory. This is possibly the oldest type of ecclesiastical court.

A metropolitan court is made up of the hierarchs composing a synod. It is the court of first instance for cases involving bishops and the court of second instance for the episcopal court.

---

136 1 Nicea 5.

137 Milaš, 669–76. Regarding spiritual courts in the Greek Orthodox Archdiocese of America, see Protocol 304, *Regulations of Spiritual Courts of the Holy Archdiocese of America*, March 20, 2014, which were issued by the Holy and Sacred Synod of Constantinople under the presidency of His All-Holiness Ecumenical Patriarch Bartholomew. These *Regulations* are included in an appendix of the companion volume, Patrick Viscuso, *Orthodox Canon Law: A Casebook for Study*, 3rd ed. (Brookline, MA: Holy Cross Orthodox Press, 2023). The translation cited in the present work is taken from that appendix.

138 For example, letters of reprimand, temporary suspension, and loss of *offikion*.

The patriarchal court is the court of highest instance for all other courts. It is made up of the hierarchs of the patriarchal synod and exists in each of the patriarchates. As a court of first instance, it tries charges against hierarchs of the patriarchate; as a court of second instance, it tries appealed decisions of the metropolitan court; and as a court of third instance, it makes final decisions on all cases brought before it from lower ecclesiastical courts.

## ECCLESIASTICAL LEGAL PROCEDURE[139]

The legal procedure by which the Church exercises judiciary authority foresees investigation of any matter of concern both on its own initiative and after a charge has been made. The involved persons include the petitioner (ἐνάγων), and respondent (ἐναγόμενος). Witnesses (μάρτυρες) may or may not be permitted. The petitioner is a person (other than a presiding hierarch or respondent), who brings an action and submits a request for convening a spiritual court. The petitioner must profess the Orthodox faith and be without accusation or a previous charge proven false. The respondent is the person, who is summoned in order to appear before the spiritual court, in order to defend himself/herself against a charge alleged against him/her regarding a disciplinary or moral offense.

The Church's legal procedure has its roots in an era when the Christian faith was not the official religion of the state. In historical cases brought before the ecclesiastical courts, the legal system was focused on protecting the rights of the faithful from the hostile intentions of non-believers. This background helps explain the requirements set out by the Church for ecclesiastical legal proceedings.[140]

The most common issues brought before an ecclesiastical court are related to the conduct of the clergy and the status of marriage.

The presiding hierarch/officer of the Spiritual Court determines the arrangement/form of the hearing procedure, not however

---

139 Milaš, 681–86.
140 Milaš, 686–92.

being limited only to it. The following form of procedure is usually observed:

(1) **Description of the Case:** The Presiding Hierarch/Officer or the person designated for this purpose by the Hierarch, from the members of the Spiritual Court or not, presents to its members a full description of the case, with a concise summary of the relevant probative evidence/supporting documentation and the available results of the investigation. The presentation takes place exclusively and only for the President and the members of the Spiritual Court.

(2) **Statements and Questioning of the Petitioner:** The petitioner is permitted to provide an opening statement and to present any additional probative evidence, after permission of the Presiding Hierarch/Officer, who, as well as the remaining members of the Spiritual Court, can put questions to him/her (the petitioner). The Presiding Hierarch/Officer can, according to his judgment, permit the petitioner to provide a possible closing statement.

(3) **Questioning of Witnesses:** The President Hierarch/Officer and the members of the Spiritual Court have the right and the capability to accept any statements of witnesses and to question each of them.

(4) **Presentation of Charges/Evidence to the Respondent:** The Presiding Hierarch/Officer, or the person designated by him for this purpose, presents to the respondent during his appearance before the Spiritual Court, a summary statement of charges as well as any other information, which he (the Presider) judges appropriate for disclosure under the circumstances under which each case is heard. A summary of the probative evidence against him/her is also made known to the respondent, unless the Presiding Hierarch/Officer may judge that such an action may impede the questioning of the respondent.

(5) **Disclosure of the Identity of the Petitioner:** The name of the petitioner (or of the petitioners) is made known to the respondent, outside of rare cases, in which the Presiding Hierarch/Officer, according to his own judgment, considers that the identity of him/her (or of them) should remain confidential, because of the specific circumstances of the case being heard or for protection of the health and security of any person.

(6) **Defense and Questioning of the Respondent:** The possibility is provided to the respondent to provide an opening statement and to provide any additional probative evidence, on the basis also of which the proceedings shall continue. The Presiding Hierarch/Officer can, according to his judgment, permit the respondent to provide a possible closing statement.

(7) **Further Questioning:** The Spiritual Court can recall any petitioner or respondent for further questioning.

(8) **Deliberations of the Spiritual Court:** After the conclusion of the hearing, while no one other is present (petitioner, respondent, witness, or any other person), the Spiritual Court deliberates privately (the presiding Hierarch being present or not, according to his judgment) and issues a written decision.

(9) **Communication of the Decisions of the Spiritual Court:** All the decisions of the Spiritual Court are made known promptly and in writing to the respondent by his/her respective Hierarch or by the one designated by him or by the Archbishop as President of the Holy Eparchial Synod, depending on the case. The communication also contains any sanction which may be placed on the respondent. The communication of the decisions to the petitioner

takes place according to the judgment of the respective Hierarch or the President of the Holy Eparchial Synod, depending on the case. The publication of the decisions of the Spiritual Court for the information of the faithful takes place consistent with the current Regulations of the Greek Orthodox Archdiocese of America.[141]

In the Greek Orthodox Archdiocese of America, the granting of an "ecclesiastical divorce," which permits remarriage in the Church, also takes place in spiritual courts known as "marriage courts," according to Protocol 304, *Regulations for Spiritual Courts of the Holy Archdiocese of America*, March 20, 2014: "Persons whose marriage was dissolved legally through civil divorce come before the spiritual court of the first instance for a decree, according to the tradition of our Orthodox Church, also of ecclesiastical divorce. This process is necessary for restoration of these persons to the sacramental life of the Church. Often, the affected individuals are not aware of the importance of this final step in the process of reconciliation with the Church, after the breakdown of marital cohabitation, and discover this necessity only during their preparation for an impending marriage being blessed by the Church."[142]

The procedures for dissolution of marriage followed in civil courts differ from those followed in Spiritual Courts of the First Instance, whose basic procedures are as follows:

1.  Marriage Courts are composed of the Presiding Hierarch/Officer and at least two (2) clergymen senior in rank, appointed by the respective Hierarch. The Hierarch or the one appointed by him (who must have the status of a clergyman) presides over the Marriage Court.

2.  The hearings before the Marriage Court often take place in a chapel or a Sacred Temple, for facilitation of the confessional character of the proceedings for the participants.

---

141 These points are taken from Protocol 304, *Regulations of Spiritual Courts of the Holy Archdiocese of America*, March 20, 2014.
142 Appendix 1, § 6, *Regulations of Spiritual Courts*.

3.  The petitioner ought to be present in person at the Marriage Court to testify and to participate in the confessional and cathartic process, outside of rare cases that are determined by the respective Hierarch.

4.  The presence of the respondent at the Marriage Court is not obligatory, but is necessary if he/she is a member of the Orthodox Church.

5.  The petitioner and respondent are called separately to a hearing by the Marriage Court, but under no circumstances are they examined at the same time.

6.  The priest of the parish of the petitioner is called to submit his pastoral evaluation and recommendation to the Marriage Court before the hearing for evaluation by it. This pastoral evaluation and recommendation constitute a necessary element available for study before the convening of the Marriage Court for a hearing of a specific case.

7.  The respective Hierarch issues the decision after the testimony and dismissal of both the petitioner and respondent (in a case where they are present). Although in most cases the decision is issued immediately, in certain cases the taking of a decision can be delayed in order that the possibility might be given of additional spiritual guidance and counsel for the petitioner or the respondent, especially if there does not exist evidence or an admission of serious moral lapses during the marital cohabitation.[143]

---

143 *Regulations of Spiritual Courts.*

## 3.2 Ecclesiastical Property Law

While penitential law provides a good example of the judiciary category of governing laws, the law of ecclesiastical property exemplifies the administrative category. Ecclesiastical property laws regulate how property is administered, and address why the Church needs property at all. This examination concerns the property of the Church in general.

The Church is both a divine institution and a human, visible institution. As such, it has need of visible and material means to realize its earthly mission. It is evident from history that individual local churches and ecclesiastical organizations possessed various kinds of property obtained from grants, gifts, and bequests. This is why it is forbidden for a bishop to make use of the property of one church for the needs of another. The same principle was adopted in Byzantine legislation, which recognized the legal right of possession by the Church and its institutions. Justinian's Novel 131 states that any bequest left to the Church becomes the property of the donor's local church.[144]

Ecclesiastical property has traditionally been acquired through the voluntary offerings of the departed faithful by legacies or bequests, and through legal acts between living persons. In the early Church, voluntary offerings took the form of the first fruits of the harvest and monetary offerings and tithes. Later, notably in the East during Byzantine times, property was acquired as a result of death through inheritance by will or by intestate inheritance.

Traditionally, the Church has acquired most of its property through bequests. A bequest differs from an inheritance in that the Church is not its possessor in the legal sense. Rather, the Church, in the person of the responsible bishop, acquires authority of supervision. The bishop is thereby invested with the authority to administer the bequest according to its intended purpose.

---

144 Justinian's Novels compose one of the four major units of Roman law initiated by Emperor Justinian I in the course of his long reign (AD 527–565). See the section above concerning sources of canonical legislation during the second period where mention is made of the significance of the contribution of the emperor Justinian the Great.

The Church may also acquire property through a legal transaction between living persons. This could take the form of gifts, donations, or the purchase of an object on behalf of the Church. This category also includes the exchange of an item for the gain of a greater benefit, such as the exchange of a building belonging to the Church for land, or acquisition of property through continual use for a lengthy period of time.[145] In more recent times, the needs of the Church have been sustained through voluntary membership offerings and acts of stewardship.

There are two categories of objects constituting ecclesiastical property: sacred objects and holy objects. Sacred objects are objects used exclusively for divine worship. They are consecrated by a special ceremony that includes anointing with holy myrrh (μύρον) and, in the case of chalices, patens, and other articles of the holy table, consecrated to the Church through sacred use. The church edifice, holy altar, holy utensils, and *antimēnsion*[146] are all examples of sacred objects. Objects sanctified by a simple blessing and kept in special storage, such as liturgical books and vestments, are also considered sacred objects. Holy objects, on the other hand, are all other objects used in sacred space but can be individually possessed such as the vestments of a priest. Sacred objects—those consecrated to the Church—are excluded from commerce or exchange, whereas objects considered holy can be privately

---

145 For instance, an item offered for use without its stipulation as a gift eventually becomes the property of the Church over time.

146 The *antimēnsion* (ἀντιμήνσιον) is a consecrated piece of cloth sometimes containing relics kept on the altar and required for celebration of the Divine Liturgy. For additional information, see Januarius M. Izzo, *The Antimension in the Liturgical and Canonical Tradition of the Byzantine and Latin Churches*, Thesis ad Lauream n. 81 (Rome: Pontificium Athenaeum Antonianum, 1975).

bought and sold.[147] The following question and answer of Theodore Balsamōn is provided for additional clarification:

## Question 3

Are the coverings for holy chalices and holy patens, and likewise other articles of the holy table, and the vessels in which holy baptisms occur, sanctified by particular prayers, or does the Communion and containing of holy things suffice for their sanctification?

## Response

It is written, 'Abraham believed in God and it was reckoned for him as righteousness.'[148] For which reason, we also believe (διὸ καὶ ἡμεῖς πιστεύομεν) chalice coverings, paten coverings, and so forth, are sanctified, at the time when they are placed on the holy altar, and cover the Holy Elements, and do not require particular prayers for sanctification. In addition, one should know that all sacred things (ἱερὰ) are holy (ἅγια), but not all holy things (ἅγια) are also sacred (ἱερὰ). For the sign of the cross on coins is holy but is not sacred. On this account, the one stealing coins that bear a venerable cross, or even the very adulated portrait of our Lord Jesus Christ, is condemned as a thief, but is not guilty of sacrilege. For chapter 1 of title 3 of book 46 of the *Basilika* clearly states, 'Sacred things belong to divine law and are not subject to ownership. A sacred thing is dedicated publicly, for things individually possessed are not sacred.'[149] At any rate, whatever is presented by anyone to the Catholic churches, or to the divine temples of monasteries, namely coverings for holy chalices and holy patens, but also any other vessels, even icons within the hands of a bishop or

147 On the other hand, certain categories of property consecrated to the Church can be sold for its benefit under certain circumstances and with hierarchical permission.

148 Gen 15:6 (LXX).

149 This is a summary of *Basilika* 46.3.1, Scheltema, A6:2124, and *Basilika* 46.3.5, Scheltema, A6:2125; cf. *Digest* 1.8.1, 6.

priest, at this point when dedicated to God they become holy and sacred (ἅγια καὶ ἱερά). Whatever such things some have in their unconsecrated oratory houses are holy (ἅγια) when they contain the Divine Sanctified Elements and are not regarded as common. They are not sacred things (ἱερὰ) because they belong to individual persons.[150]

As reported in the book of Acts, the first administrators of ecclesiastical property were the apostles themselves, striving to meet the needs of the early Christian community. Subsequently, the bishops were responsible for the administration of the Church's property as the successors of the apostles (Holy Apostles 38). As the Church's possessions increased, and in order to prevent the bishops from becoming absorbed in administrative preoccupation at the expense of their spiritual ministry, the office of *oikonomos* was introduced. Clergy who held the office of *oikonomos* were delegated by the bishop to function as stewards assigned to look after the Church's finances under his guidance (Chalcedon 26). From the time of Saint Constantine the Great, every church organization had the right to have its property administered by local clergy. In his diocese, the bishop, however, had general supervision over all ecclesiastical property and delegated its administration when appropriate.

Ecclesiastical property can be used for the construction and furnishing of churches with the necessary ecclesiastical furniture and holy utensils, for support of the clergy, for the founding of schools, and for philanthropic causes. The specific way ecclesiastical property and possessions are to be used is determined by special legislation in the various autocephalous churches.[151]

---

150 Viscuso (trans.), *Guide for a Church under Islām*, 71–72.
151 For a discussion of contemporary issues regarding property, see the article listed in Appendix B: "Parish Conflict and Parameters of Authority: A Case History."

## IV. LIFE OF THE CHURCH

The holy mysteries are classified as part of the life of the Church. They are the visible signs and means through which God's saving grace is imparted to the faithful members of the Church. This division of law includes ordination and penance, which have already been covered,[152] as well as regulations on joining the Church and on marriage.

### 4.1 MEMBERSHIP IN THE CHURCH

An individual becomes a permanent and legitimate member of the Church, while simultaneously acquiring the identity of a Christian, through baptism.[153] As its purpose is the unification and redemption of humanity, the Church invites all to become members through baptism regardless of race, gender, or social status.

The physical matter used in the performance of baptism is clear, natural water and blessed oil. The act of baptism itself is performed by triple immersion according to ecclesiastical rubric. Sprinkling is permitted only in the case of severe illness or shortage of water.

---

152 For more on ordination, see section 2.2; for penance, 3.1.
153 "Most assuredly, I say to you, unless one is born of water and the Spirit, he cannot enter the kingdom of God" (John 3:5); "He who believes and is baptized will be saved" (Mark 16:16).

The canonical sanction for clerics who violate the ecclesiastical rubric for baptism is deposition.[154]

The competent agent for performing the act of baptism under ordinary circumstances is a presbyter or bishop. Under extraordinary circumstances, as in the case of impending death, baptism can be performed by a deacon or by any Orthodox layperson who invokes the formula of the Holy Trinity.[155] Should the person receiving such a "baptism of necessity" survive, he or she must then receive the sacrament of chrismation. A cleric responsible for someone dying unbaptized, whether by negligence or indifference, is subject to canonical sanctions. A layperson responsible for the same offence is denied Holy Communion for three years.[156] Baptism performed once in a canonical manner may not be repeated. A cleric who violates the prohibition of rebaptism is to be defrocked according to canon 47 of the Holy Apostles: "Let a bishop or presbyter who shall baptize again one who has rightly received baptism . . . be deposed."[157]According to the dogmatic teaching of the Orthodox Church, martyrdom for the Christian faith, called "baptism of martyrdom" or "baptism of blood," is equivalent to the act of baptism itself.

In the ancient Church, entrance into the ranks of the catechumenate for instruction always preceded baptism. The catechumenate began to lose its importance with the appearance of infant baptism. The practice of baptizing infants first appeared during the second century and became prevalent from the fifth century on. This, together with the expansion of Christianity through the conversion of entire nations, led to the decline of the

---

154 See Holy Apostles 50 in Percival, 597: "If any bishop or presbyter does not perform the one initiation with three immersions, but with giving one immersion only, into the death of the Lord, let him be deposed. For the Lord said not, Baptize into my death, but, "Go, make disciples of all nations, baptizing them in the name of the Father, and of the Son, and of the Holy Spirit."

155 "The servant of God (N) is baptized in the name of the Father and of the Son and of the Holy Spirit." This is a variation of the received baptismal formula based on the command of Christ (Matt 28:19): "The servant of God (N) is baptized in the name of the Father, Amen. And of the Son, Amen. And of the Holy Spirit. Amen." See Trempelas, 1:360–61.

156 Mouratides, 114.

157 Percival, 597.

catechumenate. Nevertheless, catechesis continues to be applied today for adults entering the Church, and the revival of the formal catechumenate is occurring. Although infants are baptized, the catechesis of children and young adults is also a major focus of the pastoral ministry of the Church.

The presence of the sponsor at baptism also dates back to the early Church, when the initiation of adults into the Christian faith was still commonplace. At that time, it was the sponsor who guaranteed the sincere intentions and orthodox belief of the person to be baptized. With the eventual prevalence of infant baptism, the role of the sponsor was in some places reduced to the limited role of reciting the creed for the infant and making a formal promise to oversee the child's upbringing in the Orthodox faith.[158]

Obviously, even the formal role played by the sponsor in the mystery of baptism makes it absolutely necessary for him or her to be an active member of the Church. Consequently, members of another religion, heterodox individuals, schismatics, and those excommunicated are forbidden to serve as sponsors. Monastics, the parents of the child to be baptized,[159] minors, the mentally handicapped, and persons of ill repute are also forbidden from serving as sponsors.[160] If necessity demands, the sacrament of baptism may be performed without a sponsor. Although required by ecclesiastical practice, a baptism performed without a sponsor would still be recognized.

Although it is often thought that the person baptized receives his or her Christian name at baptism from the sponsor, there

---

158 The restoration of the original role of sponsors in the Orthodox Christian upbringing of their godchildren must be a goal in every priest's ministry. See Appendix B: "The Upbringing of Children in a 'Mixed' Marriage."

159 According to the *Alphabetical Collection* of Matthew Blastarēs (cited in the *Rudder*, 996), the reason a parent is prohibited to serve as sponsor to his/her own child is that the godparent is considered the spiritual brother/sister of the natural parent. For the text of Blastarēs, see Patrick Viscuso, *Sexuality, Marriage, and Celibacy in Byzantine Law*, 81.

160 Although not expressly stated in any canonical text, clergy serving as sponsors in baptism is traditionally frowned on, an impression apparently related to the impropriety of monastics serving in this capacity. In contemporary parish life, the potential for creating favored relationships with elite members of a community is evident and therefore inappropriate.

is actually a separate service for the naming of a child, which has its origins in services that are associated with the ancient catechumenate. There is a special prayer in the Euchologion,[161] "for the sealing of the child when it receives a name on the eighth day from its birth."[162] Analogous to other mysteries in the Church, formulas used in the sacraments assume that the believer is already named. For example, in marriage, "The servant of God [name] is crowned . . . ." For holy baptism, the formula is: "The servant of God [name] is baptized in the name of the Father and of the Son and of the Holy Spirit." When the name is given during the appropriate ceremony, it should belong to a saint who is commemorated by the Church. Parents are urged to limit the naming of children to one name. Under no circumstances is it permitted for names of heretics or infamous persons in history to be given.[163]

Immediately after baptism, the sacrament of holy chrismation takes place, whereby the spiritual life initiated through baptism is fortified and perfected. This sacrament, too, is performed by either a bishop or presbyter, who anoints the newly baptized person's body with holy *myron.* The ingredients comprising the holy ointment are oil and various aromatic elements. Its preparation and sanctification were originally performed by a local bishop whenever necessary. Before the end of the twelfth century, however, this became an exclusive prerogative of the ecumenical patriarch as a visible sign of his rising prestige among the other patriarchates of the East. In remembrance of this privileged status, some autocephalous churches still receive holy ointment from the Ecumenical Patriarchate. The holy ointment is consecrated and sanctified in a service performed by the ecumenical patriarch, assisted by representatives of the autocephalous churches. It takes place on Holy Thursday, usually every seven years. However, the consecration of such ointment is also performed by the primates of other autocephalous churches.

---

161 Euchologia (singular, Εὐχολόγιον; plural, Εὐχολόγια) are service books containing rites and the texts of the mysteries of the Church that are used for their celebration.

162 "εἰς τὸ κατασφραγίσαι παιδίον λαμβάνον ὄνομα τῇ ὀγδόῃ ἡμέρᾳ ἀπὸ τῆς γεννήσεως αὐτοῦ."

163 Mouratides, 116.

## ACCEPTANCE OF HETERODOX CHRISTIANS

The Orthodox Catholic Church accepts heterodox (non-Orthodox) Christians[164] into her fold with the caveat that only sacraments performed by Orthodox ministers are valid. However, for reasons of ecclesiastical expediency, the Church has revised this traditional position by applying the principle of *oikonomia*.[165]

Accordingly, leniency is shown to some heretics, depending on the content of their heresy. Arians, for example, were received into the Church only by performing the sacrament of holy chrismation, whereas Nestorians and Monophysites were received only by writing a declaration denouncing their previously held beliefs.[166] In all three cases another baptism was not required.

As for all other heresies, regardless of whether they accept the teaching of the Holy Trinity, the repetition of baptism was required.[167] Canon 95 of Trullo is the basis for this practice.

The Council of Carthage under Cyprian (256) determined that schismatics should be rebaptized. However, Saint Basil, in his canons 1 and 47, already considered this practice too severe. At the same time, canon 1 of Carthage (256) is not in harmony with canon

---

164 Despite the pejorative connotation of the term heterodox, it is used here merely to designate non-Orthodox Christians in general.

165 For an account of the way in which *oikonomia* has been applied by the contemporary Orthodox Church in America, see Appendix B: "The Application of *Oikonomia*," 153. See also the relevant decisions of the Holy and Sacred Synod of the Ecumenical Patriarchate at the end of the nineteenth century, Μιχαὴλ Θεοτοκᾶς, Νομολογία τοῦ Οἰκουμενικοῦ Πατριαρχείου (Constantinople: Νεολόγου, 1897), 370–71.

166 Although in some Byzantine commentaries, non-Chalcedonians appear to be received through abjuration of their heresy and affirmation of Orthodoxy and then application of holy *myron*. In any case, another baptism was not required. See, for example, Theodore Balsamōn's commentary on canon 14 of Chalcedon (Rhallēs and Potlēs, 2:253), where only two methods of reception are recognized, either through baptism and anointment with *myron*, or through anointment with *myron* alone.

167 See J. Erickson, "Reception of Non-Orthodox into the Orthodox Church," *Diakonia* 19, no. 1–3 (1984/85): 68–86; J. Klentos, "Rebaptizing Converts into the Orthodox Church: Old Perspectives on a New Problem," *Studia Liturgica* 29, no. 1 (1999): 216–34; and A. Calivas, "Receiving Converts into the Orthodox Church: Lessons from the Canonical and Liturgical Tradition," *Greek Orthodox Theological Review* 54, no. 1–4 (2009): 1–76.

95 of Trullo, which is lenient. It stands to reason, therefore, that schismatics should not be subjected to rebaptism when certain heretics—such as Nestorians and Monophysites, whose deviations from Orthodoxy are much more serious than schism—were only requested to sign a declaration renouncing their previously held beliefs.[168]

Bearing in mind the above canonical decrees regarding the acceptance of heterodox Christians into the Church, opinions on the baptism of heterodox churches today are as follows: The baptism of Nestorians and Monophysites is accepted; they are received into the Orthodox Church by only submitting a written renunciation of their previous affiliations, and by confessing the Orthodox faith as defined by the Council of Chalcedon.[169] Included among the latter are Armenians, Copts, Jacobites and others categorized as Monophysites or Non-Chalcedonians.[170]

The baptism of Roman Catholics is accepted. Despite doctrinal differences, they have not been declared heretics, but are treated as schismatics. For this reason, they are requested to submit a written declaration upholding the Orthodox faith and to receive the sacrament of holy chrismation.[171] The Orthodox Church applies this practice based on canons 7 of the Second Ecumenical Council and 95 of the Council of Trullo (the latter adopted and expanded the language of the former).

---

168 Mouratides, 117; see also Christophilopoulos, 2:19–20. However, see the above references regarding a diverse practice on their reception through application of holy *myron*.

169 In the Greek Orthodox Archdiocese of America, non-Chalcedonians are also received by the mystery of confession (for example, see the "Administrative Guidelines for the Mysteries of Baptism and Chrismation," 1-6, Metropolis of Denver, https://www.denver.goarch.org/documents/32140/3520504/baptism.pdf/b7c836a7-3101-4152-8354-ac1ece914612, accessed July 22, 2022, "Although Baptized Christians from the Non-Chalcedonian and Monophysite Orthodox Churches have usually been received into the Orthodox Church through the Mystery of Chrismation, they may be received through the Mystery of Confession according to Metropolitan Maximos of Pittsburgh").

170 The Council of Chalcedon (451) condemned Monophysitism, a heresy that asserted that in the person of Jesus Christ there was only one divine nature rather than two natures, divine and human.

171 See Bishop Peter, "The Reception of Roman Catholics into Orthodoxy," *St. Vladimir's Seminary Quarterly* 24 (1980): 75–82.

According to the principle of ἀκρίβεια (strictness), the baptism of certain Protestant bodies is deficient, when not performed in the name of the Holy Trinity with water and when belief in the Holy Trinity is not upheld by the denomination in question. Therefore, in the past baptism was set for converts from such groups as a presupposition for their entry into the Orthodox Church.[172] Otherwise, current practice accepts the trinitarian baptism with water conducted by mainline Protestant communions that express belief in the Holy Trinity but requires the performance of holy chrismation.

## DEPARTURE FROM THE CHURCH

According to the dogmatic teaching of the Orthodox Church, a person who has been validly baptized remains forever a member of the Church. Consequently, no matter how greatly a person has sinned or deviated from the truth of Orthodoxy by adhering to another confession—even atheistic theories—that person may still receive the gifts of divine grace upon sincere repentance without being rebaptized. However, from a legal and canonical perspective, a person's association with the visible Church can be severed by a number of causes. These include death, apostasy, and anathema. With regard to death, from a canonical perspective a deceased person is in communion with the invisible Church. Nevertheless, this person still retains certain relations with the visible Church. For example, the penalty of excommunication can be imposed posthumously, and memorial services are held for deceased members of the Church. As for apostasy, the renunciation of the Orthodox faith by a former member of the Church and adherence to another religion or to atheism, without repenting, severs that person's ties with the visible Church.[173] Similarly, the penalty of anathema or major excommunication severs one's ties with the Church for serious offenses such as heresy.

---

172 Mouratides, 118.

173 Restoration to communion with the Church by one who has committed apostasy and repented includes anointing with holy *myron*. This is seen as fortifying the faith of the repentant apostate and is indicative of the severity with which the Church views the act of apostasy.

## 4.2 LAW OF MARRIAGE[174]

### DEFINITION OF MARRIAGE

The classic definition of marriage as retained in the Orthodox Church is that of the Roman jurist Herennius Modestinus (third century): "Marriage is a union of a man and woman, a consortium of all life, and a sharing of divine and human law."[175] Three elements are named in this definition: a natural element, a moral element, and a religious-legal element. The natural element relates to the marital union of man and woman, the moral element to their shared lot (consortium) for all of life, and the religious-legal element to the communion of divine and human law.

Presuppositions for contracting a legitimate marriage under normal circumstances are: the mutual accord of the spouses, their legal age or the permission of their guardians, their mental and physical health, and their reception of an episcopal blessing for their union. Mutual accord of the spouses relates to the lifelong agreement and commitment of the spouses to uphold their sacred bond of marriage. Legal age is the age of maturity set by the state for marriage. The permission of guardians is a prerequisite in the case of those who do not meet the legal age for marriage set by the state. Mental health is considered necessary for the voluntary acceptance of marriage. Marriage is prohibited to the mentally impaired since they are incapable of appreciating the significance of their spousal obligations. This prohibition does not include persons who have only periodic mental impairment, such as those who suffer from epilepsy or memory lapses, or those with moderate intellectual disability. Similarly, marriage is also permitted to individuals with physical disabilities that do not hinder their voluntary acceptance of the marriage bond, such as deafness, muteness, or blindness.

---

174 Mouratides, 210–19; see also Milaš, 823–88.

175 "Nuptiae sunt coniunctio maris et feminae et consortium omnis vitae, divini et humani juris communicatio," *Code* 9.32.4 and *Digest* 23.2. In the Byzantine imperial code, the translation of this definition appears in Greek as, "Γάμος ἐστὶν ἀνδρὸς καὶ γυναικὸς συνάφεια καὶ συγκλήρωσις τοῦ βίου παντός, θείου τε καὶ ἀνθρωπίνου δικαίου κοινωνία," *Basilika* 28.4.1. See also Milaš, 823, quoted in Mouratides, 210.

Physical health is required of the spouses so that they and their offspring may be protected from serious illness. For this reason, a blood test for certain illnesses has been required by civil law before a marriage license could be issued. A final consideration, which stems from the time of the primitive Church, is the blessing of the bishop, known as episcopal permission. In its current form, episcopal permission dates from the time of the Byzantine Emperor Leo VI the Wise (893). It is issued once it has been determined by the hierarch that there are no impediments to the marriage.

## IMPEDIMENTS OF MARRIAGE

An impediment to marriage is a condition that hinders the contracting of marriage, or that renders illegal a marriage already performed. Impediments are either absolute or relative. Absolute impediments render a marriage invalid; relative impediments render a marriage illegal, but do not invalidate a marriage which has already taken place. Conditions considered absolute impediments include mental impairment, impotency, withholding of permission by parents or guardians (in the case of minors), pre-existing marriage, and pregnancy. In addition, ordination constitutes an absolute impediment for the married priest whose wife is deceased. Once ordained, his obligation is to his flock. Similarly, a vow of chastity from monastic tonsure prevents a monk from contracting marriage. The impediment of betrothal is only of historical significance, since today betrothal and crowning are celebrated together. Widowhood after a third marriage prevents remarriage under any circumstance, as a fourth marriage is absolutely forbidden. Finally, the conditions of deceit, force, and fear are absolute impediments depriving either one or both of the spouses from entering into marriage voluntarily, thereby violating the condition of mutual accord.

Relative impediments include lack of the age required of either spouse for marriage. This impediment is lifted automatically as soon as their legal age is reached. There are also certain days and seasons designated as inappropriate for the celebration of the wedding ceremony. Canon 52 of the Council in Laodicea sets the tone for this impediment, inasmuch as it prohibits the celebration of weddings during Great Lent. Clearly, the festivity of a wedding celebration is incompatible with the somber character of fasting seasons and fast days generally. In addition, there are feast days on which the celebration of weddings may not take place. The distraction caused by a celebratory event inappropriately detracts from the spiritual significance of the feast. Days and seasons when marriage is not permitted are Great Lent and Holy Week, Pascha, Pentecost, August 1–15 (Fast and Feast of the Dormition, Transfiguration), August 29 (Beheading of Saint John the Baptist), September 14 (Exaltation of the Precious Cross), December 13–25 (Fast and Feast of the Nativity), and January 5–6 (Theophany).[176]

Other impediments to marriage include the abusive behavior of one of the betrothed towards the other and a period of mourning for the decease of a spouse. A mourning period of one year was originally upheld for widows, to prevent any doubt of paternity in the event of childbirth during this time.

Certain personal relationships constitute impediments to marriage. Relationship in its widest sense is divided into categories of birth, marriage, spiritual bonds, and adoption. Blood relationship by birth or kinship by consanguinity is the relationship between two persons through the descent of one from the other, or through the descent of both from the same third person. This type of relationship stems from common blood bonds or consanguinity (συγγενὴς ἐξ’αἵματος), and the relatives in this relationship are called relatives "of the same blood" (ὅμαιμος).

Relationship is determined by degrees. A degree of relationship is the affinity or remoteness of relationship between two persons through a number of births. An uninterrupted succession of degrees of relationship is called a line. A line may be direct or indirect. The direct line can be an ascending line (progenitors) or a descending line (descendants). An ascending line is made up of

---

176 This is the canonical practice of the Greek Orthodox Archdiocese of America. However, Bishop Nikodim Milaš of blessed memory lists the following days in which marriage is forbidden: November 14–January 6, Great Lent through Renewal Week, the fast after the Sunday of All Saints up until June 29 (the feast of the Holy Apostles Peter and Paul), the fast prior to the Dormition of the Theotokos from August 1–15, the feast of the beheading of John the Baptist (August 29), the feast of the Exaltation of the Precious Cross (September 14), as well as Wednesdays and Fridays of the entire year (Milaš, 845).

those ascending from a certain person in direct lineage without interruption in degrees of relationship, such as father, grandfather, or great-grandfather. The descending line is composed of those descending from a certain person in direct lineage, such as son, grandson, or great-grandson.

Indirect or collateral lines are composed of persons belonging to different lines of relationship. These lines of relationship have the same source—the head of the family. Indirect relationship exists between a certain person and his or her siblings, or between this person and the descendants of his or her siblings, uncles, or aunts. In order to determine degrees of relationship, the following legal norms based on natural law are designated: a husband and wife, considered as one person, are counted as one degree of relationship to other relatives. Sons and daughters are first-degree blood relatives to their parents. Brothers and sisters with the same mother and father are second-degree blood relatives to each other. Brothers and sisters with only one parent in common are still legally regarded as blood siblings. Degrees of relationship extend to the seventh degree, beyond which intergenerational relationship is not possible according to the laws of nature.

Kinship by consanguinity was considered a marriage impediment by both Mosaic law and Roman law. It was ultimately adopted as such by canon law as well. In kinship by consanguinity, the marriage impediments of ascending and descending lines of relationship differ from those of indirect lines. In the direct line of relationship, marriage is absolutely forbidden. In the indirect or collateral line, it is forbidden up to and including the seventh degree according to strictness (κατ'ἀκρίβειαν). According to economy (κατ'οἰκονομίαν), however, marriage between spouses related in the fifth and sixth degrees can be deemed acceptable providing that circumstances warrant it.

Relationship by affinity is the relationship between two families arising through marriage. This type of relationship is divided into relationship by affinity involving two families (ἀγχιστεία ἐκ διγενείας) and that involving three families (ἀγχιστεία ἐκ τριγενείας). Διγένεια (Digeneia) arises out of the relationship between two families through one marriage. Τριγένεια (Trigeneia) arises out of the relationship among three families through two different marriages. The regulations that determine the degrees of kinship by consanguinity also apply to the degrees of relationship through marriage.

As in kinship by consanguinity, relationship through marriage distinguishes between a direct and an indirect line. Consequently, relationship through marriage may arise between the following persons: one of the spouses, and the progenitors and descendants of the other spouse; one of the spouses, and the indirect line of relatives of the other spouse; the relatives of both spouses to each other; or the relatives of one of the spouses and the relatives of the other spouse from a previous marriage (stepfather and stepdaughter).

The prohibited degrees of relationship through marriage for prospective spouses are determined by canon 87 of Saint Basil. In the direct line, marriage is absolutely prohibited, and upon the death of one of the spouses, it is prohibited for the surviving spouse to marry any of the progenitors or descendants of the deceased spouse. In the indirect line, marriage is prohibited up to and including the fifth degree (for example, marriage between second cousins) without invoking economy with episcopal approval.

Spiritual relationship is the relationship arising out of baptism between the sponsor and baptized person, as well as between certain relatives of both. This relationship is based on the regeneration of the baptized subject through baptism and the responsibility undertaken by the sponsor as the spiritual father or mother of the baptized child. According to canon 53 of Trullo, spiritual relationship is considered of greater significance than kinship by consanguinity. It was this council that determined spiritual relationship as an impediment to marriage. Due to spiritual relationship, therefore, marriage is prohibited between the following persons: the sponsor and the baptized person; the sponsor and the parent of the baptized person; the sponsor and the child of the baptized person; the child of the sponsor and the baptized person; the child of the sponsor and the child of the baptized person; and, in the past, the baptized person and any other baptized child of the sponsor.[177]

Relationship by adoption is of a legal nature and arises between the adopter and his or her relatives on the one hand, and the adopted person and his or her relatives on the other. A legally adopted person enters into the same bonds of relationship to the adopter as to his or her own blood relatives. The degrees of relationship by adoption correspond to the degrees of spiritual relationship. Impediments from the relationship by adoption originate from the Byzantine period, when the act of adoption was accompanied by a special blessing service. As this is no longer the case, impediments of adoption are limited to the adopter and adopted, and the adopted to each other.[178]

Other impediments of marriage include: abduction (ἁρπαγή);[179] adultery, if proven, constituting an absolute impediment to remarriage for the guilty party; instigation of divorce, terminating the marriage of the instigator to the person divorced; guardianship, forbidding marriage to one's guardian, or to the son or grandson of one's guardian, according to Greco-Roman law; and the difference of religion.

With regard to the last, marriage between Orthodox Christians and non-Christians is prohibited. In the early centuries of the Church's history, precedents of such marriages exist; however, although tolerated, these marriages were not formally approved. Such attempted unions were viewed as inconsistent with the third section of marriage's definition as a "sharing of divine law," namely, the spouses' sharing of one common faith.

---

177 A recent decision by the Ecumenical Patriarchate no longer considers such a relationship to be an impediment to marriage.

178 See Milaš, 880–81; and Appendix B: "Impediments of Relationship in the Sacrament of Marriage."

179 This terminology refers specifically to "abduction" as understood within the Byzantine canonical tradition. For a translation of applicable texts and canonical sources, see Patrick Viscuso, *Sexuality, Marriage, and Celibacy in Byzantine Law*, 59–63. Canons related to marriages under the pretense of abduction include canons 27 of Chalcedon, 92 of Trullo, 22 and 30 of Saint Basil, and 11 of Ancyra.

## CONSEQUENCES OF ILLEGAL MARRIAGE

Marriages attempted in violation of impediments are illegal. Illegal marriages can be incestuous/illicit, condemned, or unlawful. An incestuous or illicit (ἀθέμιτος, *incestus*) marriage is between relatives of a prohibited degree of kinship or between a Christian and a heretic. A condemned (κατάκριτος, *damnatus*) marriage is one attempted with persons consecrated to God such as monks and nuns. An unlawful (παράνομος, *nefarius*) marriage is one that social norms and certain civil laws condemned, such as marriages between guardians and their charges. Those responsible for the finances of minors were not permitted to marry them. Included in this category were also circumstances that were formerly viewed as preventing marriage because of the appearance of impropriety, such as a servant with the wife of his deceased employer.

An absolute impediment renders a marriage invalid. A prohibitive impediment renders a marriage irregular until the impediment is lifted. Once lifted, the marriage is regularized. The consequences of an invalid marriage affect not only the spouses, but also the celebrant priest and children born of the marriage. A priest who violates the prohibition by performing an unlawful marriage is released from his priestly authority. Children born of an unlawful marriage are considered illegitimate.

## DIVORCE[180]

According to the teaching of the Orthodox Church, one of the essential characteristics of marriage is its life-long nature. Consequently, a legitimate marriage is dissolved only by physical death, or by anything that revokes the ecclesiastical significance of marriage and refutes its religious and moral foundation, leading to its spiritual death.

Divorce caused by spiritual death of the marriage occurs when its basis ceases to exist and the purpose of the marital bond (δεσμός) ceases to function. Under such circumstances, there is a formal recognition that the former legitimate marriage, having lost its moral basis, has dissolved itself.

---

180 Mouratides, 219–22. See also Milaš, 896–913 and Appendix B: "The Orthodox Position on Divorce."

Marriage is the "oldest institution of divine law because it was instituted simultaneously with the creation of Adam and Eve, the first human beings (Gen 2:23)."[181] The legal basis for both marriage and divorce was established long before the Christian faith appeared. In ancient Roman society, the dissolution of marriage came about by the mutual consent of both spouses or by a formal written declaration (*libellus*) of one of the spouses indicating its dissolution.[182] With the formal recognition of the Church by the state, however, privileges were granted that accorded the institution of marriage an elevated status. At that time legislation was issued guaranteeing the sanctity of marriage. The first step taken to achieve this goal was the abolition of divorce by mutual consent. It took many centuries, however, before the Church was able to exert adequate influence on the state to abolish this type of divorce. It was not until the sixth century that canonical grounds for divorce were established with the issuance of legislation by the emperor, Justinian I the Great (r. 527–565).[183] By the ninth century, ecclesiastical wedding ceremonies were recognized by the state as having a legal character.

Grounds for granting divorce include adultery, apostasy, sponsorship of one's own child at baptism, and embracing the monastic life. Adultery is the violation of conjugal fidelity by either spouse. In view of the Church's reverence for marriage, adultery is equated to death, because it upsets the basis of the marital bond and destroys the purpose of marriage. Apostasy is the abandonment of the Christian faith by one of the spouses. Sponsorship of one's own child at baptism gives rise to the impediment of spiritual relationship between the parents of the baptized child, which is an expressly prohibited condition. Embracing of the monastic life by one of the spouses, with the consent of the other spouse, leads to a canonical dissolution of marriage by being equated with physical

---

181 Holy and Great Council (2016), "The Sacrament of Marriage and Its Impediments," I, § 2.

182 For in-depth coverage of divorce in Roman law, see Susan Treggiari, *Roman Marriage: Iusti Coniuges from the Time of Cicero to the Time of Ulpian* (Oxford: Clarendon Press, 1991), 435–82.

183 See the commentaries of Theodore Balsamōn, John Zōnaras, and Alexios Aristēnos on canon 9 of Saint Basil (Rhallēs and Potlēs, 4:121–23).

death. This is the only condition leading to divorce that is not penanced as a serious canonical violation.

Other grounds for which ecclesiastical divorce or dissolution of marriage are granted include bigamy, deceit, coercion, fear, mental disorders, impotency or a sexually transmitted disease hidden prior to marriage, abortion concealed from one's spouse, conspiracy against the life or honor of one's spouse, lengthy separation or abandonment of one's spouse without cause, crimes incurring the death penalty, immoral behavior with others, and addictions that lead to the destruction of harmonious family relationships.[184] In accordance with the 2014 legislation of the Ecumenical Patriarchate on marriage courts, "The priest of the parish of the petitioner is called to submit his pastoral evaluation and recommendation to the Marriage Court before the hearing for evaluation by it. This pastoral evaluation and recommendation constitutes a necessary element available for study before the convening of the Marriage Court for a hearing of a specific case."[185]

In the preface to the procedures of marriage courts, the same 2014 issuance states, "Persons whose marriage was dissolved legally through civil divorce come before the Spiritual Court of the First Instance for a decree, according to the tradition of our Orthodox Church, also of ecclesiastical divorce. This process is necessary for restoration of these persons to the sacramental life of the Church. Often, the affected individuals are not aware of the importance of this final step in the process of reconciliation with the Church, after the breakdown of marital cohabitation, and discover this necessity only during their preparation for an impending marriage being blessed by the Church."[186]

---

184 Many of these grounds were developed in ecclesiastical legislation received by the Church, such as the rulings of Holy Synods, based on the legislation of Justinian I the Great (r. 527–565).
185 Appendix 1, § 6, *2014 Regulations of Spiritual Courts*.
186 Appendix 1, *Regulations of Spiritual Courts*.

## EXCEPTIONAL MARRIAGE[187]

According to the uninterrupted teaching and tradition of the Church, a first marriage is considered canonical and holy. A second marriage is exceptional, permitted by *oikonomia* and in a spirit of compassion because of human frailty. As defined by the rubrics for the celebration of a second marriage (*digamy*), those who marry a second time ought not to be crowned during the wedding ceremony, as are those married only once. However, this tradition has been applied inconsistently in Church practice. In the history of the Great Church of Christ in Constantinople, even second unions were at times crowned.[188]

The austerity of the Church is greater towards those who marry a third time. Saint Basil refers to third marriages as "pollutions."[189] Nevertheless, as a concession to human weakness and the desire for procreation, the Church allowed marriage for a third time to those above the age of thirty who did not have children and others below forty, even with offspring, who desired a third union. Permission for such marriages, however, was granted under the condition that the parties involved be subject to ecclesiastical penance and continued restrictions from Holy Communion involving lengthy periods of fasting. A fourth marriage was forbidden. The *Tomos of Union*, the canonical legislation regarding these provisions on third and fourth marriages, was issued by the local council of Constantinople in 920.[190] Fourth marriages continue to be prohibited and are invalid if performed in violation of the *Tomos*.

---

187 Milaš, 913–15.

188 See Patrick Viscuso, *Sexuality, Marriage, and Celibacy in Byzantine Law*, 32–34.

189 Saint Basil 50 (Rhallēs and Potlēs, 4:203).

190 The local council of 920 resolved the canonical and theological dispute in the Byzantine Church that resulted from the attempted fourth marriage of Emperor Leo VI (r. 886–912). The dispute was resolved with the promulgation of the *Tomos of Union* that formulated the decisions of the local council. The critical edition of the *Tomos* is found in L. G. Westerink, ed. and trans., *Nicholas I Patriarch of Constantinople: Miscellaneous Writings* (Washington, DC: Dumbarton Oaks, 1981), 58–69.

## MIXED MARRIAGE[191]

A mixed marriage refers to the marital bond between two persons of different Christian faith. According to strictness (ἀκρίβεια), canon 72 of the Council in Trullo forbids the marriage of an Orthodox Christian to a non-Orthodox Christian. However, such marriages with a baptized non-Orthodox Christian are permitted in North America through the application of *oikonomia*. The current guidance is contained in the *Guidelines for Orthodox Christians in Ecumenical Relations*, published in 1973 by the former Standing Conference of Canonical Orthodox Bishops in the Americas (SCOBA).[192] This application of *oikonomia* permits such unions with the understanding that there be no agreement in place before the marriage that excludes the possibility of raising the children in the Orthodox faith. The *oikonomia* is understood as applied in a limited way to the non-Orthodox spouse in that they are not otherwise able to participate in other mysteries of the Church. The current practice of permitting mixed marriages must eventually be addressed by a pan-Orthodox council.[193]

---

191 Milaš, 916–19. See also Appendix B: "'Mixed' Marriages and the Canonical Tradition of the Orthodox Church," "A Canonical Response to Intra-Christian and Inter-religious Marriages," and "Interchurch Marriages: An Orthodox Perspective."

192 SCOBA was dissolved in 2010 and its ministries were assumed by the Assembly of Orthodox Canonical Bishops of North America.

193 The issue of mixed marriages was taken up by the 2016 Holy and Great Council of Crete; however, it did not reach a unanimous decision regarding a justification for uniformity of practice. Instead, it recognized the right of each autocephalous church to make that determination based on its own local circumstances. For a recent discussion of mixed marriage, see Anthony Roeber, *Mixed Marriages: An Orthodox History* (Yonkers, NY: Saint Vladimir's Seminary Press, 2018).

# V. GOVERNANCE OF THE LOCAL CHURCH

The local church as understood in this context is the Greek Orthodox Archdiocese of America. It is one of several Orthodox Church jurisdictions in America and is governed by principles of the holy canons and canonical tradition, reflected in its charter.

## 5.1 HISTORY OF THE GOVERNANCE OF THE GREEK ORTHODOX ARCHDIOCESE OF AMERICA[194]

The Greek Orthodox Archdiocese of America,[195] with headquarters in New York City, is an eparchy of the Ecumenical Patriarchate of Constantinople, incorporated in 1921. Since then, it has been governed according to the charters granted to it by the Church of Constantinople. Its current charter, the fifth in succession since its incorporation, was granted by the Holy Synod of the Patriarchate in 2003. Each of the five charters reflects the needs of the archdiocese during different phases of its growth and development. These phases necessitated drastic changes in its administrative structure. The characteristic adaptability of the Orthodox canonical tradition enabled the continuing unity of the Greek Orthodox Archdiocese of America throughout these changes. This necessary flexibility

---

194 Section 5.1 is a lightly edited version of a previously published work, found in Appendix B: "History of the Governance of the Greek Orthodox Archdiocese of America." It has been reprinted here with permission.
195 Hereafter, "the archdiocese."

and prioritization of unity explain the variations in governance evident since the inception of the archdiocese.

Like the statutes regulating the synodal structure of the various local (autocephalous) Orthodox churches,[196] ecclesiastical charters are also of recent conception. In order to understand their significance, one must first appreciate the role of statutes. Each local Orthodox church follows its own statute, which applies the principles found in the ancient canons to the concrete requirements of church life in specific parts of the world. Statutes are, for the most part, an attempt to cast the living practice of the Church into clearly defined procedures. This was made necessary by the relations between church and state at the time of their adoption.[197]

A similar need exists for an ecclesiastical charter. It helps clarify the role of the religious body for which it is issued. The charter of the archdiocese, issued by its Mother Church, the Ecumenical Patriarchate of Constantinople, is the document that defines its manner of operation in America.

The first four charters (1922, 1927, 1931, and 1977) of the archdiocese reveal the stages of its history up to the current Charter of 2003. An overview of their contents may prove helpful in understanding what led to its present administrative status.[198]

## CHARTER OF 1922

The year after the incorporation of the archdiocese in 1921, its first charter was granted. It is composed of twenty-seven articles that define the purpose of the archdiocese and articulate how this

---

196 Collections of the ancient canons, accompanied by commentaries, are the basis of the contemporary statutes which each autocephalous Orthodox church follows in applying the principles of the canons to its governance. See J. Meyendorff, "Contemporary Problems of Orthodox Canon Law," in *Living Tradition* (Crestwood, NY: St. Vladimir's Seminary Press, 1978), 102.

197 See Appendix B: *Primacy and Conciliarity*, 32–34.

198 For a detailed analysis of the charters of the archdiocese, see Appendix B: "History of the Charters," from which some of the material in this paper originates.

purpose is to be achieved.[199] As stated in Article 2, its purpose is to nurture the religious and moral life of American citizens of the Orthodox faith, who are either themselves Greek or of Greek ancestry.[200]

Article 3 establishes the relationship of the archdiocese to the Ecumenical Patriarchate.[201] This is a supervisory relationship based on canonical and historical right. The following article delineates the geographical boundaries of the archdiocese.[202] They outline four diocesan districts: New York (chief see of the archdiocese and headed by an archbishop), and Chicago, Boston, and San Francisco (each headed by a bishop bearing the name of his see).

By introducing these four sees, the archdiocese initially sought to establish itself on the American continent with a traditional synodal form of governance. It thereby remained faithful to the principle of conciliarity. Later, however, it was compelled by circumstances to deviate for a time from this authentic model of canonical administration.

In the Charter of 1922, the archbishop and three bishops make up the synod of the Greek Archdiocese of North and South America. The synod of the archdiocese has all the authority and responsibility inherent in the "provincial synod," as defined by the holy canons. It is accountable to the Holy Synod of the Ecumenical Patriarchate for the inviolate preservation of the doctrines and canons of the Orthodox Church.[203]

Each diocese has its own ecclesiastical assembly composed of all the clergy of the diocese and of one lay representative from each incorporated parish. Ecclesiastical assemblies are convened by the diocesan bishop—its presiding officer—or his representative. These assemblies are empowered to supervise the management of

---

199 Due to the unavailability of an official translation of the first three charters (1922, 1927, and 1931) in English, texts used, with modifications, are those appearing in Rodopoulos, 223–48.

200 Rodopoulos, 223 (Charter of 1922, Article 2).

201 Rodopoulos, 223 (Charter of 1922, Article 3).

202 Rodopoulos, 224 (Charter of 1922, Article 4).

203 Rodopoulos, 226 (Charter of 1922, Article 7).

all ecclesiastical affairs and to enact legislation together with the local bishop for the effective administration of all ecclesiastical institutions.[204]

The general assembly of the entire archdiocese is composed of the archbishop, bishops, clergy, and lay representatives of each of the four local ecclesiastical assemblies. It is presided over by the archbishop or, in his absence, by the bishop with seniority of consecration. The general assembly reaches decisions and approves measures that foster common action throughout the archdiocese towards achieving its stated religious, moral, and social goals.[205]

Within the archdiocese and each of the three dioceses there is an executive council. The executive council of the archdiocese is composed of the archbishop, who is its presiding officer, four clergy, and four lay representatives. The executive council of each of the dioceses is composed of the bishop with only three clergy and three lay representatives. The jurisdiction of the executive council includes all matters for which the entire represented body is competent. These do not include matters that are canonically the exclusive privilege of the bishop, acting alone or in concert with the spiritual court of the diocese. The executive council, under its presiding bishop, also has the right to enact legislation within the sphere of its jurisdiction that does not conflict with the present charter.[206]

Each diocese has its own spiritual court of at least two presbyters and the local presiding bishop or his representative. This court hears all canonical offenses of the clergy in the first instance, with exception of offenses for which defrocking/deposition is foreseen. These are referred to the synod of the archdiocese.[207]

In accordance with the holy canons, the archbishop and bishops are permanently installed and cannot be transferred. In the event the archiepiscopal see becomes vacant, one of the three remaining bishops may be elected archbishop. Because the newly established

---

204 Rodopoulos, 228–29 (Charter of 1922, Articles 12, 15).
205 Rodopoulos, 228–29 (Charter of 1922, Articles 13, 15).
206 Rodopoulos, 230–31 (Charter of 1922, Articles 20, 21).
207 Rodopoulos, 227 (Charter of 1922, Articles 10, 11).

archdiocese had only an archbishop at the time, it was necessary to fill the additional three vacant sees of Chicago, Boston, and San Francisco. Consequently, an established procedure for the initial election of bishops for the three newly created dioceses was adopted. It requires the convening of the ecclesiastical assembly by the archbishop. Its purpose is to propose three candidates from an approved list, of whom one is elected bishop by the Holy Synod of the Ecumenical Patriarchate.[208]

Once the three vacant sees have been filled in this way, vacant sees in the future will be filled by a similar procedure. Here, too, the charter calls for the ecclesiastical assembly to propose three candidates from a pre-approved list. In contrast to current practice, however, it foresees the election of each bishop, or in the case of the archdiocese, the archbishop, by the synod of the archdiocese and the ratification of the election by the Holy Synod of the Ecumenical Patriarchate.[209]

The charter concludes by asserting the right of the clergy of the archdiocese to be assigned to their ministerial posts without the interference of the civil authorities. Furthermore, it affirms that the bases for all administrative procedures are the holy canons, the regulations adopted in accordance with them, and the laws of each state where the Church's jurisdiction extends.[210]

Besides the synodal structure of governance in this first charter, the participatory role of the laity is also notable. This role is reflected primarily by lay representation in the several administrative bodies introduced. It is also in keeping with the premise that, although hierarchical, the Church is made up of both clergy and laity, who together express her essence when acting synergistically.[211] These characteristics—a synodal form of governance and lay participation—will continue to be upheld.

---

208 Rodopoulos, 229–30 (Charter of 1922, Article 16).
209 Rodopoulos, 230 (Charter of 1922, Article 17).
210 Rodopoulos, 231–32 (Charter of 1922, Article 24).
211 Regarding a synergistic approach involving both clergy and laity in the governance of the Church, see Appendix B: *Spiritual Dimensions of the Holy Canons*.

## CHARTER OF 1927

Within five years, a revision of the Charter of 1922 took place. There is little difference in language between the original charter and the newly revised Charter of 1927. The revised charter is a refinement of the original and includes new provisions, which ensure a more effective operation of the administrative structure of the archdiocese. Its intention is not to introduce a new administrative structure, but to apply recent experience in anticipation of future developments of the Greek Orthodox Church in America. For instance, its purpose was revised, as stated in Article 2. Not only is it to preserve and propagate the Orthodox Christian faith, but also to teach the original language of the Gospel.[212] Such an expanded purpose was an indication of the growing awareness that the Greek Orthodox Church in America was there to stay and needed to plan for the future.

The geographical boundaries of the archdiocese remain the same and include the four diocesan districts, as in the earlier charter. Mention is made of existing communities as well as those to be established in the future, another indication of the Church's anticipation of a permanent presence and further growth in America.[213] As the 1927 charter is mostly a refinement of the previous charter, there are no substantive changes introduced. Where there are changes, they serve to clarify or expand on policies or procedures in corresponding articles of the earlier charter.

With regard to both the local and general ecclesiastical assemblies with lay representation, the 1927 charter calls for greater precision in their composition. A wide variety of possible candidates is suggested. These include members of the parish council or of the community, as well as Orthodox Christians of another city or of the city in which the ecclesiastical assembly takes place. It is of utmost importance that candidates be in good standing with the Greek Orthodox Church.[214]

---

212 Rodopoulos, 233 (Charter of 1927, Article 2).
213 Rodopoulos, 233–36 (Charter of 1927, Article 4).
214 Rodopoulos, 238–39 (Charter of 1927, Articles 13, 14). See also Appendix B: "History of the Charters," 79–80.

A precise definition of good standing with the Church is not articulated. It must be assumed that this refers to membership in the Church in both a broad and narrow sense. In a broad sense, one is a member of the Church through baptism and subsequent communion in the faith; in a narrow sense, by meeting financial and other obligations determined by the local parish. Stressing good standing with the Church multiple times as a prerequisite for membership in an ecclesiastical assembly is revealing.[215] It is likely that this was the direct result of the turbulence that had begun to ravage the Greek Orthodox Church in America at this time.[216]

In order for the charter of any parish to be valid, it must be ratified by the local bishop.[217] This requirement is especially significant when seen in the light of the turbulent events of this period, as it was necessary to consolidate parishes under the authority of the bishop. It appears, in fact, to have been a measure taken to strengthen the bishop's authority, which might otherwise be challenged by those seeking parochial autonomy.[218]

The procedure established in the previous charter for the election of both the archbishop and bishops is retained in the Charter of 1927.[219] An additional qualification for either of these offices, understandably absent earlier, is the requirement for a fruitful ministry in the Church in America of at least five years for bishops and seven years for the archbishop. However, in the case of the archbishop, candidates may also be selected from among current metropolitans of the Ecumenical Throne who might not have served the Church in America. Once again, the election of

---

215 Rodopoulos, 238–39 (Charter of 1927, Articles 13, 14, 15).

216 For an historical account of the formative years of the Greek communities in America, see G. Papaioannou, "The Historical Development of the Greek Orthodox Archdiocese of North and South America," in *A Companion to the Greek Orthodox Church*, ed. F. Litsas (New York: Greek Orthodox Archdiocese of North and South America, 1984), 178–206. See also Βασίλειος Θ. Ζούστης, Ὁ ἐν Ἀμερικῇ Ἑλληνισμὸς καὶ ἡ δρᾶσις αὐτοῦ, Ἡ Ἱστορία τῆς Ἑλληνικῆς Ἀρχιεπισκοπῆς Ἀμερικῆς Βορείου καὶ Νοτίου [*Hellenism in America and Its Activity: The History of the Greek Archdiocese of North and South America*] (New York: D. C. Divry, Inc., 1954), 105–8, 113–15.

217 Rodopoulos, 240 (Charter of 1927, Article 16, § 1).

218 See Appendix B: "History of the Charters," 81.

219 Rodopoulos, 240–41 (Charter of 1927, Article 18).

each bishop, or of the archbishop, takes place from among three candidates by the synod of the archdiocese and is ratified by the Holy Synod of the Ecumenical Patriarchate.[220]

The 1927 charter concludes with a reminder to both clergy and laity of what otherwise might appear self-evident: "Neither cleric or layperson may hold office or even be a member of the Greek Orthodox Church of America if that person does not belong to the Orthodox Church of Christ, and none may remain in office or even be a member of the Church in America if that person ceases to be in good standing with it."[221] The need to return to the issue of good standing addressed earlier[222] strongly suggests the persistence of abusive activity leading eventually to the next charter.

## CHARTER OF 1931

The Charter of 1927 was short-lived. The subsequent Charter of 1931[223] guided the administration of the archdiocese for forty-six years, until 1977. The Charter of 1931 cannot be appreciated without knowledge of events surrounding the life of the newly established Greek Orthodox Church in America at that time. An investigation into the early years of its existence reveals a period of instability and division.[224] Waves of immigrants from Greece, seeking a new life in America, brought with them the political rivalries of their homeland. As a result, communities were divided, and the legitimacy of the existing ecclesiastical authority was contested. Clergy of questionable credentials, ordained by bishops

---

220 See Appendix B: "History of the Charters," 81.

221 Rodopoulos, 242 (Charter of 1927, Article 27).

222 Rodopoulos, 238–39 (Charter of 1927, Articles 13, 14, 15).

223 For a negative reaction to this document, see J. Counelis, "Historical Reflections on the Constitutions of the Greek Orthodox Archdiocese of North and South America, 1922–1982," in *Workbook of the 26th Biennial Clergy-Laity Congress* (San Francisco: n.p., 1982), 39–40. For a chronology of events leading up to the displacement of the two previous charters by the Charter of 1931, see Ζούστης, Ὁ ἐν Ἀμερικῇ Ἑλληνισμὸς καὶ ἡ δράσις αὐτοῦ, 193–207.

224 The turbulence of this period is graphically portrayed in a lecture by Peter T. Kourides, long-standing legal counsel of the archdiocese, and published as a booklet with the title *The Evolution of the Greek Orthodox Church in America and Its Present Problems* (New York: Cosmos Greek-American Printing Company, 1959), 7–11.

of opposing factions, contributed to the already chaotic situation permeating the Church in America.[225]

This was the situation encountered by the visionary Archbishop Athenagoras (later ecumenical patriarch), who in 1931 arrived on the American continent as the new spiritual leader of the Greek Archdiocese. His perseverance and vision, as well as his administrative ability, contributed significantly to the eventual stabilization of the Church's affairs. Seeds of dissension had been scattered long before his arrival. Consolidation of authority into one source to preserve unity therefore appeared necessary. The cause of unity must indeed have been the main concern of those responsible for drafting the new charter. It would be difficult, otherwise, to understand the drastic departure of its monarchical model of administration from the synodal model of the two earlier charters.[226]

An immediately notable aspect of the Charter of 1931 is the absence of the mention of dioceses. The only administrative unit mentioned is the archdiocese. The archdiocese is headed by the archbishop, for whom an auxiliary bishop is foreseen to assist in administrative duties. Both the archbishop and auxiliary bishop proposed by him are elected by the Holy Synod of the Ecumenical Patriarchate.[227]

In the absence of a synod, all authority is centralized in the person of the archbishop. Details of the operation of the archdiocese are to be contained in regulations that supplement the articles of the charter. These regulations, together with the charter, play an important part in the orderly administration of the archdiocese from here forward. They are to be drafted by committees that are appointed and chaired by the archbishop and are binding after their ratification by the Ecumenical Patriarchate.[228]

Regulations defining details of operation are foreseen for eleven articles of the charter. Among them are Article 8, which announces

---

225 Regarding the status of Greek immigrants and their parishes in America, see Thomas Fitzgerald, *The Orthodox Church* (Westport, CT: Praeger Publishers, 1998), 25–7.

226 See Appendix B: "History of the Charters," 82–83.

227 Rodopoulos, 245 (Charter of 1931, Articles 6, 7).

228 Rodopoulos, 247 (Charter of 1933, Article 17).

the establishment of an archdiocesan office as yet undefined,[229] and Article 9, which mentions the creation of ecclesiastical assemblies to assist in the realization of the archdiocese's purposes.[230]

Of singular significance is the mixed council introduced in Article 10. It, too, assists in the realization of these purposes, especially in the management of ecclesiastical property and the establishment of funds to meet the needs of the church and the clergy.[231] In order to locally achieve the goals outlined for the mixed council, the parish council is introduced to function as a local community affairs council.[232] Given the tumultuous situation that led to the new charter, this seems to have been a measure introduced to promote stability on the local level.

In accordance with the stated purpose of the archdiocese, several newly established institutions are officially sanctioned by the charter. They include Missions, a Board of Higher Education, and a Department of Religious Education. Mention is also made of spiritual courts and of ecclesiastical authorities dealing with matters of marriage and divorce.[233]

According to Article 19, the assignment of clergy to their ministerial posts is the inherent right of the canonical and lawful ecclesiastical authority of the archdiocese.[234] The need to affirm this claim is an indication of the uncanonical activity of the unauthorized hierarchs that contributed to the prevalent instability. There follows the same prohibitive statement made earlier in the Charter of 1927[235] regarding those persons, clergy or lay, who are not in good standing with the Church. They may neither serve in any office nor be a member of the archdiocese.[236]

The concluding article makes reference to the 1931 charter's composition according to provisions made in the Charter of 1927 and confirms its ratification and validation by the Holy Synod of

---

229 Rodopoulos, 245 (Charter of 1931, Article 8).
230 Rodopoulos, 245 (Charter of 1931, Article 9).
231 Rodopoulos, 245–46 (Charter of 1931, Article 10).
232 Rodopoulos, 246 (Charter of 1931, Article 11).
233 Rodopoulos, 246–47 (Charter of 1931, Articles 12, 13, 14, 15, 16).
234 Rodopoulos, 247 (Charter of 1931, Article 19).
235 Rodopoulos, 238–39 (Charter of 1927, Articles 13, 14, 15).
236 Rodopoulos, 247 (Charter of 1931, Article 20).

the Ecumenical Patriarchate. In addition, it allows for possible amendments in non-essential provisions to be initiated by a special committee appointed by the archbishop and requiring ratification by the Patriarchate.[237]

## CHARTER OF 1977

The Charter of 1977 was the result of efforts begun several years earlier to decentralize the archdiocese's cumbersome administrative system. Over the years since the Charter of 1931, the Greek Orthodox Church in America had expanded in a way the original immigrants might never have thought possible. With this expansion, the weighty responsibilities of its chief hierarch, the Archbishop of North and South America, grew also.

The initial solution to the problem of administering an ecclesiastical province of such an unprecedented geographical size was to assign several auxiliary bishops to assist the archbishop in the execution of his administrative duties. The Charter of 1931 foresaw one auxiliary bishop.[238] By 1977, the number of auxiliary bishops had increased to ten. As assistants to the archbishop without full episcopal authority, they had only the right to execute his administrative decisions within their archdiocesan districts.

The Charter of 1977 was a bold attempt to adjust to the growing needs of the Church of the late twentieth century. These needs demanded a participatory form of administration consistent with the conciliar nature of the Church. It was therefore timely and necessary that the restoration of a synodal form of governance should be initiated.

A comparison of the Charter of 1977 to the previous charters of the archdiocese reveals an increasing awareness of the Church's mission in the western hemisphere. The first two charters speak of outreach to Orthodox of Greek ethnicity alone.[239] The Charter of 1931 leaves open the possibility of including a much broader membership.[240] The Charter of 1977 speaks specifically of "[embracing] within its spiritual aegis and administration other

---

237 Rodopoulos, 247–48 (Charter of 1931, Article 22).
238 Rodopoulos, 245 (Charter of 1931, Article 6).
239 Rodopoulos, 223 (Charter of 1923, Article 2), 233 (Charter of 1927, Article 2).
240 Rodopoulos, 244 (Charter of 1931, Article 2).

Orthodox groups, parishes and dioceses that have voluntarily submitted to (the) jurisdiction (of the Archdiocese of North and South America) subject to the approval of the Ecumenical Patriarchate."[241] Also characteristic of the 1977 charter is the pastoral tone of its stated purpose and its reference for the first time to engagement in inter-Christian and inter-religious ecumenical activities. It thereby commits the Greek Orthodox Church in America to dialogue and involvement in the ecumenical movement based on the directives of the Ecumenical Patriarchate.[242]

Assisting in the administration of the newly expanded role of the archdiocese are the ecclesiastical assemblies and councils, composed of both clergy and laity, encountered in the three previous charters. The most significant feature of the 1977 charter is the restoration of the synod of bishops after forty-six years, which functions as a modified provincial synod.[243]

The most important modification of the provincial synod's traditional prerogatives concerns the election of the archbishop and bishops. The election of the archbishop is the exclusive privilege of the Holy Synod of the Ecumenical Patriarchate. In this process, the synod of bishops and the archdiocesan council also have an advisory voice.[244] In the election of bishops, the synod of bishops, in consultation with the archdiocesan council, nominates three candidates from among whom one is elected bishop by the Holy Synod of the Patriarchate.[245]

As indicated, the decentralization of the administrative structure of the archdiocese is the main contribution of the Charter of 1977. This was accomplished primarily by restoring the collective authority of the synod of bishops and the individual authority of each bishop in his own diocese. The rights and responsibilities previously accorded only to the archbishop are now shared with

---

241 Rodopoulos, 249 (Charter of 1977, Article 4).
242 Rodopoulos, 249 (Charter of 1977, Article 2).
243 Rodopoulos, 250 (Charter of 1977, Article 6).
244 Rodopoulos, 252 (Charter of 1977, Article 13).
245 Rodopoulos, 253 (Charter of 1977, Article 14).

the bishops. A provision of the charter, however, modifies the extent of their episcopal authority.[246]

This provision is intended to promote initiative at the diocesan level while preserving the bond of unity that has sustained the life of the archdiocese. In it, the archbishop retains the right to supervise and coordinate the rights and responsibilities of the bishops with those of the archbishop.[247] This charter seeks the ideal balance of authority between the archbishop and bishops. There must be a modus operandi that allows the bishop to initiate needed change, while taking into account the responsibility of the primate for the general well-being of the Church at large. This model of governance, introduced by the 1977 charter, was the beginning of a transitional period of decentralization.[248]

As in the previous three charters, the laity is well represented in the administrative bodies of the archdiocese. These include the clergy-laity congress and archdiocesan council on the level of the archdiocese, and the clergy-laity assembly and diocesan council on the level of the diocese. In these bodies, the laity cooperates with the clergy in significant administrative matters such as the designation of diocesan sees[249] (subject to approval of the Ecumenical Patriarchate), and has an advisory role in the election of the archbishop and bishops.[250] The Charter of 1977 thus affirms the need for greater participation of the laity in the organizational life of the Church.

## CHARTER OF 2003

The concluding article of the Charter of 1977 is exclusively devoted to the issue of revision "as the need therefore arises."[251] The current Charter of 2003 was the result of the lengthy process that led to the transition from a synod of bishops, functioning as a modified provincial synod, to a fully functional eparchial synod with the

---

246 Rodopoulos, 251 (Charter of 1977, Article 8). See also Appendix B: "History of the Charters," 88.
247 Rodopoulos, 250 (Charter of 1977, Article 7).
248 See Appendix B: "History of the Charters," 88.
249 Rodopoulos, 249 (Charter of 1977, Article 4).
250 Rodopoulos, 252–53 (Charter of 1977, Articles 13, 14).
251 Rodopoulos, 255 (Charter of 1977, Article 24).

archbishop as president and metropolitans as its members. In the words of Archbishop Demetrios, the former archbishop of America, "This Charter honors our Archdiocese by elevating our Dioceses into Metropolises of the Archdiocese, and by enhancing our participation in the process of the election of the Archbishop and the Metropolitans. In addition, the co-operation between clergy and laity and their harmonious function within the Church is clearly affirmed throughout the various articles of the new Charter."[252]

The needs of the Church in the contemporary world were already apparent with the approach of the third millennium. They are reflected in a report prepared in 1988 by a commission appointed by the Archbishop of North and South America at that time, Archbishop Iakovos. The commission "was assigned the task of reflecting on the factors behind the identity crisis [within the Orthodox Church], formulating clear responses and offering recommendations pertaining to the priorities of the Archdiocese."[253]

Although acknowledging that the 1977 charter made an important contribution by restoring a synodal form of governance, the report raised questions about authority and leadership in light of new challenges facing the Church. The charter's lack of clarity about the highest practical authority in the archdiocese raised further questions concerning structure and organization. These included the extent of authority in certain roles, the issue of lay participation, and the nature of archdiocesan relations with other Orthodox canonical jurisdictions in America.[254]

With regard to the issue of authority, the relationship of the synod of bishops to both the archdiocesan council and clergy-laity congress was considered to be unclear. It was necessary, therefore, to clarify where the authority of one body ended and the authority

---

252 Letter of Archbishop Demetrios, *Charter of the Greek Orthodox Archdiocese of America*, Greek Orthodox Archdiocese of America, 2003.

253 *Report to His Eminence Archbishop Iakovos Concerning the Future Theological Agenda of the Greek Orthodox Archdiocese* (Brookline, MA: Holy Cross Orthodox Press, 1990), 2.

254 *Report to His Eminence Archbishop Iakovos*, 14.

of the other began. Similarly, the relationship of the bishops to the archbishop was identified as a matter to be addressed.[255]

According to the report, lack of a clear understanding of the modified role of diocesan bishops in the 1977 charter gave them the appearance of bureaucrats. This perception was sometimes enhanced by the insistence on unimportant bureaucratic procedures within their dioceses. Furthermore, this lack of clarity created tension in the relations of the bishops with the archbishop. Such tension might manifest itself in the confusion of rights and responsibilities exclusive to the archbishop and those reserved for the bishops, thus jeopardizing the unity of the archdiocese.[256]

The continued absence of regulations defining the role and operating procedures of spiritual courts, the archdiocesan council, and diocesan councils hindered the effective functioning of these bodies. It also allowed for decisions to be reached without full participation of all parties involved.[257] The report also emphasized the need of guidelines in harmony with the work of the clergy and based on the model of the early Church.[258] Too often, laypersons serving in important decision-making bodies of the archdiocese had a deficient knowledge of the faith. This created a false impression about the role of lay participation in the Church and was the cause of serious problems in many parishes during their formative years.[259]

The report also contained positive information. Especially encouraging was the reminder that the Greek Orthodox Archdiocese is not the only Orthodox canonical jurisdiction within the geographical boundaries of America. The report acknowledges that there are differences among the canonical jurisdictions, but that all share in the ecclesial reality that is Orthodoxy. Furthermore, it stresses that "differences [must] be transformed into a common loyalty to Christ, a shared love for one another, and the sense of a unified Orthodox Christianity in common service." It then

---

255 *Report to His Eminence Archbishop Iakovos*, 14.
256 *Report to His Eminence Archbishop Iakovos*, 15–16.
257 *Report to His Eminence Archbishop Iakovos*, 16.
258 See 1 Cor 12:12–31.
259 *Report to His Eminence Archbishop Iakovos*, 17.

identifies the need to cultivate the cause of pan-Orthodox unity on the level of the local parish as well as on the level of relations among the bishops of all the jurisdictions.[260]

It should be noted that the current Charter of 2003 pertains only to the territory of the United States. In 1996, the Ecumenical Patriarchate divided what had been the Archdiocese of North and South America into four eparchies (United States of America, Canada, Central America, and South America). This change necessitated the process of updating the charter. As stated at the time, "The proposed Charter has been carefully designed to provide a framework for the structure of the Greek Orthodox Archdiocese today as well as for its mission in the foreseeable future." Attention was given to points of concern related to specific articles of the new 2003 charter. They consisted of an affirmation of the integrity and unity of the archdiocese and its bond to the Ecumenical Patriarchate, of issues related to the election of the archbishop, the metropolitans, and the auxiliary bishops, and of the extensive lay participation in the administrative process of the archdiocese.[261]

The process of the report leading to the 2003 charter revealed much about the level of maturity of the Greek Orthodox Church in America.[262] The new charter's ultimate purpose was to strengthen

---

260 *Report to His Eminence Archbishop Iakovos*, 17–18.

261 "The Proposed Charter: Progress and Potential," *Orthodox Observer* 67, no. 1189 (May 2002): 1, 3.

262 Regarding the drafting of the Charter, "Questions and Answers on the New Charter" that were posted on the Greek Orthodox Archdiocese of America website at the time stated the following (http://www.goarch.org/archdiocese/documents/charterpage/char_qa, accessed July 29, 2022): "What was the process of preparing the new Charter? The new Charter was prepared over an extensive period of time by a Joint Archdiocesan/Patriarchal Committee, a process that included the participation of our Synod, our Clergy-Laity Congress, our Archdiocesan Council, our Parishes, and our people throughout the Church in America. The text was distributed in advance of and reviewed at the 2002 Congress in Los Angeles. All opinions, ideas, suggestions, and comments were reviewed in the process, carefully documented, and forwarded to the Patriarchate for consideration prior to the granting of the Charter. In addition, the complete transcript of the seven hours of charter discussions of the 2002 Congress was also sent to the Patriarchate. All in all, the process of preparing the Charter has been a remarkable spiritual achievement for which as Orthodox Christians we are deeply thankful to God."

the bond of unity between the Ecumenical Patriarchate and the Greek Orthodox Archdiocese of America. This led to an improved text that addressed issues not included in the 1977 charter (metropolitans, auxiliary bishops, monasteries, etc.). In addition, it opened the way for the revision of the all-important Regulations of the Archdiocese. These regulations relate to the work of the eparchial synod, the role of clergy-laity congresses, and the function of councils, assemblies, and parishes of the archdiocese. Finally, the text of the new charter upholds the necessity of having both clergy and laity administer the archdiocese. As a result, it seeks to enhance the synergy between clergy and laity in a common focus on the mission of the Church in the new millennium.[263]

The observations and concerns that led to the revision of the previous Charter of 1977 are an indication of the Church's flexibility when necessary. This flexibility is reflected in the introduction to the current Charter of 2003 by Ecumenical Patriarch Bartholomew:

> The Mother Church has chosen and adopted from the suggested proposals [for changes in the Charter] the ones that contain in themselves a prudent, reasonable and gradual transformation of current provisions. A primary aim in this task was offering the possibility to the whole body of the Archdiocese of an orderly ascent to new provisions, so that when the proper time comes and adjustment to the new conditions is successfully achieved, the Mother Church will proceed to offer other possible changes, if the conditions at that time show that such changes are useful for a desirable further development and progress in Christ of the Holy Archdiocese of America.[264]

Each of the charters of the archdiocese addressed the needs of its era. Their goal must always be the preservation of unity, a goal requiring flexibility to achieve and adaptability to retain. These characteristics have allowed the Greek Orthodox Archdiocese of America to observe its centennial anniversary in 2022.

---

263 "The Proposed Charter: Progress and Potential," 1, 3.
264 Patriarchal Letter, *Charter of the Greek Orthodox Archdiocese of America*, Greek Orthodox Archdiocese of America, 2003.

# VI. RELATIONS OF THE CHURCH TO NON-ORTHODOX CHRISTIANS

Within the contemporary Orthodox Church globally, there are varying views regarding relations of Orthodox and non-Orthodox Christians. Orthodox Christians living in nontraditional Orthodox lands in recent years have been presented with the challenge of interacting in practice and dialogue with their brothers and sisters of other Christian faiths. What follows is a brief reflection on the theological premise of this challenge. For further enlightenment on this topic, Appendix A, directly following, contains the practical guidelines adopted by Orthodox jurisdictions in America, which outline appropriate relations in the search for reconciliation.

## 6.1 ORTHODOXY AND ECUMENISM[265]

In his prayer for the Church that was to be, our Lord asked that all the Church's members might be one, just as he and his Father are one (John 17:11, 21–23). Where there are divisions, where there is exclusiveness, where there is competition, the cause of Christianity is harmed, and the prayer of our Lord hindered. As our Lord saw

---

265 Section 6.1 is a slightly edited reprint of an earlier publication on this topic. See Appendix B: "Orthodoxy and Ecumenism."

it and prayed for it, it was to be our unity that would convince the world of the truth of Christianity and of the place of Christ.

We have tragically strayed from this vision of the Church. Faced with the disunity of Christians, the world cannot see the supreme value of the Christian faith. It is, therefore, our individual duty to demonstrate that unity of love towards one another that is the response to our Lord's prayer. If our quest for unity is correctly undertaken and guided—if our response to the urgings of the Holy Spirit is profoundly right and true—if we are unbending in zeal and unfailing in love—then, in God's providence, and in God's own time, we will be led to the fullness of our unity.

Commitment to this firmly held belief has characterized the involvement of the Orthodox Church in ecumenism for over half a century. The first official ecclesiastical document to reflect this was the encyclical letter issued by Ecumenical Patriarch Joachim III, in 1902:

> The union... of all who believe in Christ with us in the Orthodox faith is the pious and heartfelt desire of our Church and of all genuine Christians who stand firm in the evangelical doctrine of unity, and it is the subject of constant prayer and supplication;... If, as in every matter which is impossible with men but possible with God, we cannot yet hope for the union of all as ever being a possibility, yet because divine grace is constantly active..., one must consider very carefully whether it might be possible to prepare the (at present) anomalous way which leads to such a goal..., whereby might be fulfilled... our Lord and God and Savior Jesus Christ's saying about one flock and one shepherd.[266]

This same commitment was reaffirmed by the much-acclaimed encyclical issued by the Patriarchate of Constantinople in 1920 and again by the encyclical of 1952.

What is that unity of which these documents speak? How ought it to be understood? It is a unity in the totality of faith. Orthodox

---

266 Constantin G. Patelos, ed., *The Orthodox Church in the Ecumenical Movement* (Geneva: World Council of Churches, 1978), 30–31.

teaching on this point has been consistent. First and foremost, it stresses what unity in the totality of faith is not. It is neither the fusion of heterogeneous elements, nor the abandonment by force of each church's individual characteristics, nor a new mixture of different concepts foreign to the Church's age-old tradition.

Furthermore, unity in the totality of faith is not expressed in isolation by bishops or theologians or even local councils, but by the only competent body reflecting the conscience of the Church—an ecumenical council. Unity in the totality of faith concerns not only two local churches that may have entered into consultations, but all churches they have communion with. This becomes apparent when reference is made, for example, to the Church of Constantinople and the Church of England. The Church of Constantinople is only one of the communion of Orthodox churches and the Church of England is only one of the church bodies of the worldwide Anglican Communion. From an Orthodox perspective, any decision affecting the permanent relations of these two churches ultimately affects all the churches with which each is in communion.

The union of two churches is not a matter of the beliefs of many or few individuals on either side coinciding, but of identical faith existing in the entire body of both of them. Unity, therefore, is a matter of proximity to spiritual truth. The closer we are to the truth contained within the Church, the closer we are to one another. In the words of the Russian theologian Alexis Khomiakov: "It is not possible for the Church to be the sum total of all the Orthodox, Latins, and Protestants. It is nothing if there does not exist total internal harmony of faith and external harmony of expression, notwithstanding local variations in worship."[267]

Restated affirmatively, Khomiakov's words call to mind "the goal of visible unity in one faith and in one Eucharistic fellowship expressed in worship and in common life in Christ" appearing in the Constitution of the World Council of Churches. Yet in order for this goal ever to become a reality, it will be necessary—in the words of the encyclical of 1920—"above all, (that) love should be rekindled and strengthened among the churches, so that they should no more

---

267 Quoted in W. J. Birkbeck, *Russia and the English Church* (London: Rivington, Percival & Co., 1895), 69–70.

consider one another as strangers and foreigners, but as relatives, and as being a part of the household of Christ and 'fellow heirs, members of the same body and partakers of the promise of God in Christ' (Eph 3:6)."[268]

The Orthodox Church has been involved in the work of ecumenism from its early years. This is not to say that all the local churches within Orthodoxy have always been equally committed to ecumenism. The historical experience of some has caused them to proceed with much caution. One cannot fault them for this, for it is strongly upheld in Orthodoxy that unity does not necessarily require uniformity. Consequently, each local Orthodox church has the right to determine the extent of its participation in ecumenism, and some resistance can have occasional benefit as a guard against mere sentimentality.

On a positive note, Orthodox living in lands where they constitute a minority take their lead from the example of the Ecumenical Patriarchate of Constantinople, which is the first ranking church of Orthodoxy. Conscious of its responsibility to worldwide Orthodoxy, which emanates from its historical role, the Church of Constantinople has sought to separate the past from both the present and future. This is not an easy task; but methodologically, it does work. It has in fact been pointed out that one reason why the North American continent provides such fertile ground for ecumenism is that its participants are free from the biases promoted by a preoccupation with the past. The Church of Constantinople, despite many and serious difficulties, has consistently taken the lead in promoting ecumenism.

There is much to be said about the involvement of the Orthodox Church in ecumenism. First, no church can be truly ecumenical without the presence of the tradition of Eastern Christianity it represents. Second, contacts with representatives of Western Christianity permit it to have a fuller appreciation of the variety of traditions within the Christian Church. This compels the church to re-examine its own tradition in the light of these contacts

---

268 Birkbeck, 69–70.

with other Christians. Such a re-examination leads inevitably to a better understanding of its own tradition, which can then be more effectively conveyed to others.

In the final analysis, we know all too well the ways that we are divided, and this causes us pain, as it should. But we do not know all the ways that we are united. Our Lord asked that we might be one, just as he and his Father are one. This prayer should sustain our hope in achieving the goal of ecumenism, but it should also inform all our efforts. If we truly seek unity, we must learn to love it. We have so much to learn from one another about what each has done and what each has become under the guidance of the Holy Spirit. As we are reminded in the encyclical of the Ecumenical Patriarchate of 1920: "For if the different churches are inspired by love, and place it before everything else in their judgments of others and their relationships with them, instead of increasing and widening the existing dissensions, they should be enabled to reduce and diminish them."[269]

---

269 R. Stephanopoulos, *Guidelines for Orthodox Christians in Ecumenical Relations* (New York: SCOBA, 1973), 28.

# APPENDIX A.
# GUIDELINES FOR ORTHODOX
# CHRISTIANS IN ECUMENICAL RELATIONS[270]

These *Guidelines* were published by the Standing Conference of Canonical Orthodox Bishops in America (SCOBA), the body that preceded today's Assembly of Canonical Orthodox Bishops of the United States of America. They were commended to the clergy for guidance in their relations with non-Orthodox Christian communions. Although issued almost fifty years ago, their directives are as applicable today as then.

## WORSHIP WITH NON-ORTHODOX

1. The Orthodox Church makes a clear distinction between liturgical and non-liturgical prayer. Our liturgical prayer is the prayer and devotional action of the holy Orthodox Church. In this sense, liturgical prayer is the official prayer of the Orthodox Church and is to be conducted according to the forms, prescriptions and canons of our Church.

2. Non-liturgical prayer can be understood in two senses. In one sense, it is the private prayer or devotions of the faithful

---

270 Reprinted from R. Stephanopoulos, *Guidelines for Orthodox Christians in Ecumenical Relations* (New York: SCOBA, 1973), 13–23 with permission.

Orthodox. In this sense, it is also the prayer of the Church and has ecclesial character and significance, insofar as one prays within the context and life of the Church. In another sense, however, non-liturgical prayer may be understood as that private or corporate prayer of divided Christians from diverse communions who come together, not as the Church, but as separated brethren seeking Christian unity. It is common prayer of non-ecclesial character. It is to be prudently used within the context of the ecumenical movement and the pluralistic setting of our society.

3. The basic Orthodox conviction has always been that unity at the altar, the unity of the members of the Orthodox Church, is a gift of God. The celebration of the Holy Eucharist and the reception of Holy Communion in the Divine Liturgy is the final end and goal of the Christian life, the very fulfillment of unity. All of the services and prayers of the Church are intimately connected with the Liturgy and express that gift of unity which is given to us by God and preserved in the bonds of faith and love. Therefore, the services of the Church are restricted to the members of the Orthodox Church and must not be understood or implemented as means toward that unity. As a sacramental community of faith and grace, the Orthodox Church in its self-understanding and with full responsibility for the Apostolic Faith which has been entrusted to it, encourages liturgical worship and frequent participation in the sacraments for its own members. At the same time, it encourages non-liturgical prayer for the union of all people, for peace, reconciliation and the spirit of charity.

4. In the interests of sharing our spiritual heritage, non-Orthodox may be invited to attend Orthodox liturgical services. It should be made absolutely clear, however, that no *communicatio in sacris* is intended or implied by such attendance. The same is true for those Orthodox who for reasons of family unity, courtesy, the demands of public life, or a deeper appreciation of the worship of other

communions might be invited to attend a non-Orthodox denominational service. In extending or accepting such invitations, care should be taken not to offend against the regulations or sensitivities of other communions.

5. Clergy of other communions attending Orthodox services may be welcome as guests of honor, and given some special place within the *solea*. High dignitaries of other Churches, when the formal occasion indicates, might be seated adjacent to the Bishop's throne when a Bishop is present. Civic authorities may be seated in the first rows or opposite the Bishop's throne on the *solea*.

## SPECIAL COMMON PRAYER PRACTICES

1. A clergyman is free to accept invitations to observances of a civic, patriotic or general community nature. If invited to offer a prayer at such an observance, e.g., school commencement, Independence Day, Memorial Day, Veterans Day, banquets, United Nations observance, etc., conducted in a public place or a neutral hall, the participating priest may accept the invitation but should not wear any form of liturgical vestment. The prayer should be composed for the occasion by the priest, reflecting the Orthodox attitude toward the issue as found in our Service Books, but also respecting the spiritual sensibilities of all the participants who are inevitably of diverse backgrounds.

2. In services of an interfaith or interreligious nature, e.g., national feasts, public calamity and mourning, Brotherhood Week, the dignity of the family, expressions for peace, justice and the like, whether in a public building or a religious edifice, a form of dress which is neither liturgical nor merely civil, viz. the *rasson* (cassock) may be considered appropriate, together with pectoral cross (if so entitled), or academic dress when indicated. No part of the liturgical vestments, such as stole, is proper.

3.  "Ecumenical services" refer to forms of non-liturgical worship or devotion mutually acceptable to all participating parties in which Christians of various communions take part. Although such services are concerned particularly with the restoration of Christian unity, they may be held for any common concern in which Christians can and should cooperate with one another.

4.  "Ecumenical services" may be conducted in an Orthodox Church with the permission of the Bishop. Furthermore, Orthodox Christians may take part in such services in the churches of other communions, as well as in other appropriate locations.

    a)  In order to avoid any misunderstanding, however, these services should be publicly acknowledged and identified as "ecumenical" in character, emphasizing the firm Orthodox position that these are prayers for unity, and not services of the one Church.

    b)  An Orthodox priest should not wear liturgical vestments at such services. The *rasson* and pectoral cross (if so entitled), or academic dress are appropriate.

    c)  If invited to participate, the Orthodox priest should share in the preparation and planning for an "ecumenical service" and contribute to its proper form and content. Prayers and petitions from the Orthodox Service Books are recommended.

d)  When "ecumenical services" are conducted in an Orthodox Church, the host Pastor may compose an appropriate service based on the prayers and forms of the Orthodox Service Books. Clergy and laity of other communions may be invited to read the Scriptures, offer prayers and give invocations. Clergy of other communions may be invited to preach. All such services in an Orthodox church must take place outside the *ikonostasion*, in the area of the *solea*. Occasions for "ecumenical services" are usually provided during the Week of Prayer for Christian Unity (January 18–25); the days from Ascension to Pentecost; and on the occasion of meetings or other events of ecumenical origin serving an ecumenical purpose. Although petitions and prayers for unity are a regular part of the Orthodox liturgical practice, "ecumenical services" may be encouraged as a means of sensitizing our faithful to the tragedy of Christian disunity and developing the spirit of charity, understanding and prayer for all persons.

e) Orthodox clergy and laity are free to read Scriptures, offer prayers, and give invocations at "ecumenical services." Likewise, Orthodox clergy may preach on these occasions.

5. A special service for the Week of Prayer for Christian Unity has been prepared by an Orthodox Committee. It is as follows:

1. Blessed be our God . . .
2. Heavenly King, Comforter . . .
   Trisaghion . . .
3. Come let us worship . . .
   Psalm 102
4. Great Litany
5. Psalm 145
6. Only Begotten Son and Word of God . . .
7. Beatitudes
8. Prescribed Scriptural Readings
9. The heavenly choir praises Thee and sings:
   Holy, Holy, Holy . . .
10. Nicene Creed
11. Release, remit, and forgive . . .
12. Our Father . . .
13. Kontakion of the Elevation of the Cross
14. Kyrie eleison (12 times)
15. May the name of the Lord be blessed . . .
    Glory, and now . . .
16. Psalm 33
17. Dismissal

## PREACHING ON ECUMENICAL OCCASIONS

1. It is evident that only a duly authorized Orthodox Christian may preach in the framework of the Divine Liturgy. The Divine Liturgy is a closed eucharistic assembly being restricted to the active participation of Orthodox Christians alone. The sermon or homily is directed to the upbuilding of the congregation, and is intended to be a clear exposition of the Orthodox teaching. The preacher is entrusted to proclaim the Apostolic Faith in the name and under the authority of the Bishop.

2. Although non-Orthodox are welcome to attend a celebration of the Divine Liturgy and may even be given places of prominence in the congregation, they are not permitted to read the Scriptures or to preach during the celebration. For any exceptions to this regulation, the Bishop must be consulted.

3. Basic to correct relations with clergy of other communions is the *principle of reciprocity*. Stated plainly, this means that in extending an invitation, a person is prepared to receive one, and conversely, accepting an invitation implies readiness to extend one. Generally speaking, if we are unable to reciprocate an invitation, we should not accept one. There are obvious exceptions to this, of course, but when in doubt it is best to consult one's ecclesiastical superior.

4. Opportunities are often provided at "ecumenical services" for preaching. Should an Orthodox clergyman be invited to preach a sermon, his acceptance must be conditioned by two considerations: first, that this ecumenical service be clearly identified as such and not be construed as a Eucharistic celebration; and second, that he be free to reflect the mind and teaching of the Orthodox Church in his sermon.

5. An invitation to preach at a non-Orthodox confessional service may be accepted by an Orthodox priest, provided he remains free to reflect the mind and teaching of the Orthodox Church in his sermon.

## SACRAMENTS AND OTHER LITURGICAL SERVICES

### I. HOLY EUCHARIST

1. Unity in the faith and the active life of the community is a necessary precondition to sharing in the sacraments of the Orthodox Church. The Standing Conference of Canonical Orthodox Bishops in America has expressed the clear position of the Orthodox Church throughout the ages:

   "To the Holy Communion the Church admits only her baptized and chrismated children who confess the full Orthodox Faith, pure and entire, and by it she shows forth their oneness with her and with her Divine Spouse. Holy Communion is the sign and evidence of right belief and of incorporation in the Israel of God. Further, the Church teaches that the Eucharist cannot be found, and must not be sought outside the covenanted mysteries. It is the achievement of unity.

   "The Standing Conference would at this time remind the children of the Church as they pray, study and work for Christian reunion that the Eucharistic Mystery is the end of unity, not a means to that end, and that therefore, the decisions regarding Holy Communion reached by Christian bodies outside the Orthodox will have no significance or validity for the Orthodox Church or her members. Holy Communion will not be sought by Orthodox Christians outside of the Church, nor will it be offered to those who do not yet confess the Orthodox Church as their mother."

2. This position must be made explicit by the Orthodox pastors whenever a question may arise of a disciplinary or ecumenical nature. It has been solemnly affirmed in the bilateral conversations of the Orthodox representatives with Roman Catholics, Episcopalians, Lutherans, and Reformed Christians, and has been officially promulgated in the findings and statements of these bilaterals.

## II. BAPTISM

1. In the Sacrament of Baptism, a person is incorporated into the crucified, resurrected and glorified Christ and is reborn to participate in the divine life. Baptism is necessary for salvation and in accordance with Tradition must be performed by triple immersion in the Name of the Father, the Son and the Holy Spirit, according to the form in the Service Book. It is conferred only once.

2. In the event of an unbaptized infant near death, an Orthodox priest must be called for a clinical baptism. Instructions for the performance of a clinical baptism may be obtained from the Bishop's office.

3. In the absence of an Orthodox clergyman, an Orthodox layman or any other Christian may baptize the infant by the sprinkling of water, repeating the formula "The servant of God, (N.) is baptized in the name of the Father, of the Son and of the Holy Spirit."

4. When receiving into the Orthodox Church a person who comes voluntarily from another confession, the Orthodox priest will accept the candidate by means of whichever of the three modes prescribed by the Sixth Ecumenical Council is appropriate (Canon 95):

   a) Baptism by triune immersion;
   b) Chrismation;
   c) Confession of faith.

5. Proof of the fact of baptism must be established by an authentic document or by the testimony of a qualified witness. The priest must undertake to instruct the applicant in matters of the Faith and practice that govern the inner life and outward behavior of the Orthodox Christian. If the applicant has not been baptized in the Name of the Holy Trinity in a Christian church whose baptism could be accepted in the Orthodox Church by the principle of *oikonomia*, he or she must be baptized as prescribed in the Service Books. In cases of doubt, reference to the Bishop is mandatory.

## III. CHRISMATION

1. Chrismation is normally administered immediately after the Rite of Baptism as contained in the Service Book.

2. An applicant from another Christian community who has been baptized already in the Name of the Holy Trinity may be received into the Orthodox Church according to the order prescribed by the Bishop.

3. The name of the person received into full communion with the Orthodox Church by means of baptism, chrismation or a confession of faith is to be entered into the parish Baptismal Records under the day of the rite together with the date and place of the Baptism of the person.

4. Because the Sponsor or Godparent at a Baptism or Chrismation service participates liturgically and canonically in the sacrament and because he or she assumes the obligation to provide for the Christian formation of the baptized as a representative of the Orthodox community of faith, standing as a sponsor for the faith of the candidate, members of communions other than the Orthodox Church may not act as sponsors in an Orthodox baptismal or chrismation service. Conversely, Orthodox Christians may not act as sponsors in baptism or confirmation in non-

Orthodox communions. Orthodox priests should explain carefully to the faithful the evangelical and ecumenical reasons for this regulation so that all misunderstanding of it may be prevented. This regulation does not apply to friends or relatives who may wish merely to witness or to be present at such ceremonies.

## IV.   MARRIAGE

1. Normally, the Sacrament of Marriage in the Orthodox Church takes place only between members of that Church. The Orthodox teaching emphasizes the positive aspects of marriage and family life, concentrating on the mutual spiritual growth and fulfillment of the partners and on their obligations to nurture their children in the Orthodox faith. To be in proper canonical and spiritual standing, an Orthodox Christian must be married in the Orthodox Church.

2. In our pluralistic society it is inevitable that an increasing number of persons will enter into marriage with a partner that is from a different religious tradition. *Mixed marriages,* for a variety of spiritual and socio-psychological reasons, are not to be encouraged. Orthodox Pastors are obliged to explain the serious responsibilities and difficulties involved in mixed marriages.

3. By application of the principle of *oikonomia,* the Orthodox sacrament of marriage between an Orthodox and a Christian baptized in the Name of the Holy Trinity may be performed in the manner prescribed in the Service Book. The Orthodox sacrament is not permitted in the case of two non-Orthodox Christians or in the case of an Orthodox and an unbaptized person. The Pastor must point out the spiritual peril in these cases to the engaged couple and urge that an acceptable solution be found.

4. Following proper pre-marital instruction and after having satisfied all the legal and canonical requirements, an Orthodox marriage must ordinarily take place in the Church according to the prescribed form of the Service Book, the Orthodox priest being the sole celebrant. Permission to perform this sacrament in another church building or in some neutral place must be granted by the Bishop.

5. In the event of a mixed marriage, double performances in both the Orthodox Church and some other Church are not to be encouraged, except when it is required by the necessity of regularizing the proper canonical standing of the Orthodox spouse.

6. The intimate relation of the sacraments to the community of faith and grace precludes the participation of non-Orthodox in their celebration. We have already indicated that by *oikonomia* a mixed marriage may be performed for the sake of the Orthodox party. *Oikonomia* does not apply, however, to anyone other than the non-Orthodox Christian party in the marriage. This prohibition applies particularly to non-Orthodox clergymen and Sponsors in the strict sense.

7. Priests should endeavour to meet the clergy of other communions to explain the theological and pastoral reasons for the Orthodox Church's canonical regulations on marriage, and, at the same time, to become familiar with the marriage regulations of other communions. This assists in promoting mutual understanding, if not mutual agreement.

8. Should the parties in a mixed marriage request the presence of a non-Orthodox clergyman, the following should be made clear:

   a) The Orthodox pastor will issue an invitation to the clergyman;

   b) The Orthodox ceremony does not permit the active participation of non-Orthodox clergy, this being made explicit to all concerned;

   c) At the conclusion of the Orthodox ceremony, the guest clergyman, advised as to appropriate vesture and as agreed previously, will be properly acknowledged. If he desires, he may give his benediction to the couple and address to them words of good wishes and exhortation;

   d) Announcement and publication of the marriage should indicate clearly the distinction between the celebrant and the guest clergyman, avoiding such terms as "assisted" or "participated."

9. If an Orthodox priest is invited, he may attend the marriage ceremony in a non-Orthodox Church as a guest.

10. As in the case of baptism and chrismation, the Sponsoring witness (Best Man) at an Orthodox marriage must be an Orthodox Christian. Non-Orthodox persons may act as witnesses, ushers or bridesmaids at the Orthodox ceremony. This applies to the Orthodox who may wish to act as attendants at marriages properly solemnized in other religious communions.

11. In the case of marriages involving Orthodox and Roman Catholic Christians, it should be noted that the spirit of the Vatican Decree on the Eastern Churches recognizes the validity of the marriage of the Catholic party if performed in the Orthodox Church. Orthodox pastors are enjoined to call this to the attention of Roman Catholic officials in order that fewer misunderstandings arise and that proper dispensation be secured.

12. It is the obligation of the parents to nurture their children in all things. The religious education of children is the right and the responsibility of both parents. It cannot be totally limited to one or the other parent. Pastors should respect the conscience of both parties in their plans for the religious rearing of their children. No prior agreement which would exclude the possibility of raising the children in the Orthodox Faith should be entered into by the Orthodox party. Every reasonable effort should be made to raise the children as Orthodox Christians.

## V.   ORDINATIONS

1. During Ordinations, Christians of other communions may be invited to attend for reasons of friendship, courtesy or ecumenical interest. They cannot be invited to take an active part in the Liturgy.

2. If they are clergymen, they could be given a special place of honor within the church (the exact place and mode of dress to be determined in advance, in each instance).

3. Although Orthodox Christians may not take an active role in the ordinating or installation ceremonies of other churchmen, they may accept for reasons of friendship, courtesy or ecumenical interest, invitations to be present for these ceremonies, although only with *rasson*. An Orthodox clergyman should consult with his Bishop before accepting such an invitation.

## VI. CONFESSION AND HOLY UNCTION

1. The sacraments are a means of divine grace and a sacred activity of the community of faith, celebrated within the community and symbolizing the oneness in faith, worship and life of the community. Where this unity is incomplete, the participation of the non-Orthodox is not permitted. For the same reason, an Orthodox Christian may not participate in the sacraments or ordinances of other communions.

2. In the extreme case that a non-Orthodox person, being without access to the ministrations of his own faith-community, summons an Orthodox priest and declares his faith to be in harmony with that of the holy Orthodox Church, his or her confession may be heard and the sacraments of Baptism, Chrismation, Holy Unction and/or Holy Communion administered with the understanding that he or she is joining the Orthodox Church.

## BLESSINGS, HOSPITAL MINISTRATIONS AND CHAPLAINCIES

1. When visiting a hospital, prison, home for the aged, or other similar institutions, an Orthodox priest should not hesitate to bless or pray with members of other faiths and communions who make such a request. It should be understood that visitations to hospitals and other such institutions, for the purpose of seeking out and ministering to the spiritual and other needs of the Orthodox patients, are a normal part of his routine duties.

2. Every effort should be made to inform the authorities of these institutions both administrative and chaplains, of the presence and availability of the nearest Orthodox clergyman for spiritual and sacramental ministrations.

3. Orthodox chaplains in the armed forces or on the staff of schools, colleges and medical and social services institutions are to be advised by the general guidelines contained herein. Particular problems should be directed to the Bishop's attention.

## FUNERALS AND MEMORIAL SERVICES

1. Orthodox burial services are normally conducted for Orthodox Christians in regular canonical and spiritual standing with the Church.

2. There is precedent and provision in the Service Book for burial of non-Orthodox persons under certain conditions. However, this dispensation is not a general one and ought not to be applied without consultation with the Bishop.

3. An infant of an Orthodox family who has not been baptized may be buried by an Orthodox priest with special prayers as follows:

   Blessed be our God . . .
   Holy God, Holy Mighty . . . (3)
   Our Father . . .
   O God of spirits and of all flesh . . .
   For thou art the resurrection . . .
   Epistle and Gospel of the Burial service . . .
   Dismissal and Internment

4. *Memorial Services* are offered normally according to the form of the Service Book for Orthodox Christians who have been buried in the Church. In doubtful cases, the Bishop should be consulted.

# APPENDIX B.
# RELATED PUBLICATIONS OF THE AUTHOR

*Listed alphabetically*

"The Application of *Oikonomia*: The Experience of the Orthodox Church in America." *Kanon* 24 (2016): 152–69.

"A Canonical Response to Intra-Christian and Inter-religious Marriages." *Greek Orthodox Theological Review* 40, no. 3–4 (1995): 287–98.

"The Canonical Tradition of the Orthodox Church." In *A Companion to the Greek Orthodox Church,* edited by F. K. Litsas, 137–47. New York: Greek Orthodox Archdiocese, 1984.

"Diaspora vs. Local Church/Churches: The Specific Problems of America." *Kanon* 22 (2012): 69–79.

"Ecclesiastical Reform: At What Cost?" *Greek Orthodox Theological Review* 40, no. 1–2 (1995): 1–10.

"The Harmonization of Canonical Order." *Journal of Modern Hellenism* 19–20 (2001–2002): 211–28.

"History of the Charters." In *History of the Greek Orthodox Church in America,* edited by M. B. Efthimiou and G. A. Christopoulos, 67–92. New York: Greek Orthodox Archdiocese, 1984.

"History of the Governance of the Greek Orthodox Archdiocese of America." *Kanon* 25 (2019): 407–23. An edited version of this has been reprinted here with permission.

"Impediments of Relationship in the Sacrament of Marriage." In *Servant of the Gospel: Studies in Honor of His All-Holiness Ecumenical Patriarch Bartholomew*, edited by Thomas FitzGerald, 139–57. Brookline, MA: Holy Cross Orthodox Press, 2011.

"Interchurch Marriages: An Orthodox Perspective." Co-authored with Charles Joanides. *International Academy for Marital Spirituality Review* 6, no. 2 (2000): 215–21.

"The Interface of Pastoral Ministry and the Holy Canons." *Kirchenrecht und Oekumene: Festgabe Panteleimon Rodopoulos*, special issue, *Kanon* 15 (1999): 179–95.

"Lived Experience and Theoretical Differences in the Approach to Law and Discipline in the Eastern and Western Churches." In *Rightly Teaching the Word of Your Truth*, edited by N. M. Vaporis, 185–202. Brookline, MA: Holy Cross Press, 1995.

"*Miscellanea Canonica*: Responses to Canonical Irregularities." In *Studies in Orthodox Hermeneutics: A Festschrift in Honor of Theodore G. Stylianopoulos*, 451–78. Brookline, MA: Holy Cross Orthodox Press, 2016.

"'Mixed' Marriages and the Canonical Tradition of the Orthodox Church." *Greek Orthodox Theological Review* 23, no. 3–4 (1978): 243–56.

*A Noble Task: Entry into the Clergy in the First Five Centuries.* Brookline, MA: Holy Cross Orthodox Press, 2007.

"The Orthodox Position on Divorce." *Diakonia* 5, no. 1 (1970): 4–15.

"Orthodoxy and Ecumenism." *Ecumenism* 77 (March 1985): 3–5. Reprinted here in a slightly edited form.

"Parish Conflict and Parameters of Authority: A Case History." In *Legacy of Achievement: Festal Volume for Metropolitan Methodios of Boston*, edited by George Dion Dragas, 670–83. Brookline, MA: Greek Orthodox Metropolis of Boston, 2008.

*Primacy and Conciliarity: Studies in the Primacy of the See of Constantinople and the Synodal Structure of the Orthodox Church.* Brookline, MA: Holy Cross Orthodox Press, 1995.

"The Primacy of the See of Constantinople in Theory and Practice." *Greek Orthodox Theological Review* 37, no. 1–4 (1992): 233–58.

"The Relationship between the Clergy and the People from a Canonical Perspective." *Ortodoksia* 2, no. 3 (1994): 576–89.

"The Spirit of Compassion in the Canonical Tradition of the Church." In *Violence and Christian Spirituality*, edited by Emmanuel Clapsis, 303–9. Geneva: WCC Publications, 2007.

*Spiritual Dimensions of the Holy Canons.* Brookline, MA: Holy Cross Orthodox Press, 2003.

"The Synodal Structure of the Orthodox Church." *St. Vladimir's Theological Quarterly* 39, no. 1 (1995): 71–98.

"Theological and Canonical Understandings." In *Role of Priest and Apostolate of Laity*, edited by N. M. Vaporis, 13–23. Brookline, MA: Holy Cross Orthodox Press, 1982.

"The Upbringing of Children in a 'Mixed' Marriage." *The Word* 23, no. 5 (1979): 8–9.

# BIBLIOGRAPHY

*For works by the author, see Appendix B.*

Afanasiev, Nicholas. "The Canons of the Church: Changeable or Unchangeable?" *St. Vladimir's Theological Quarterly* 11 (1967): 54–68.

Agapios Hieromonk and Nikodēmos Monk. *The Rudder (Pedalion) of the Metaphorical Ship of the One Holy Catholic and Apostolic Church of the Orthodox Christians.* Translated by D. Cummings. Chicago: The Orthodox Christian Educational Society, 1983.

Ἀλιβιζάτος, Ἀμίλκας [Alivizatos, Amilkas]. "Ἡ Συνείδησις τῆς Ἐκκλησίας" [The Conscience of the Church]. *Ἐπιστημονικὴ ἐπετηρὶς τῆς Θεολογικῆς Σχολῆς τοῦ Πανεπιστημίου Ἀθηνῶν* 10 (1954).

Birkbeck, W. J. *Russia and the English Church.* London: Rivington, Percival & Co., 1895.

Calivas, A. "Receiving Converts into the Orthodox Church: Lessons from the Canonical and Liturgical Tradition." *Greek Orthodox Theological Review* 54, no. 1–4 (2009): 1–76.

Χριστοφιλόπουλος [Christophilopoulos], A. *Ἑλληνικὸν ἐκκλησιαστικὸν δίκαιον* [*Greek Ecclesiastical Law*]. 3 vols. Athens: Ἐκδοτικὸς Οἶκος Δημ. Ν. Τζάκα–Στεφ. Δελαγραμμάτικα, 1954–1956.

Counelis, J. "Historical Reflections on the Constitutions of the Greek Orthodox Archdiocese of North and South America, 1922–1982." In *Workbook of the 26th Biennial Clergy-Laity Congress*. San Francisco: n.p., 1982.

Eichmann, Eduard and Mörsdorf, Klaus. *Lehrbuch des Kirchenrechts auf Grund des Codex Iuris Canonici*. 10th ed. Paderborn: Verlag Ferdinand Schöningh, 1959.

Erickson, J. "Reception of Non-Orthodox into the Orthodox Church." *Diakonia* 19, no. 1–3 (1984/85): 68–86.

Fitzgerald, Thomas. *The Orthodox Church*. Westport, CT: Praeger Publishers, 1998.

Florovsky, Georges. "The Function of Tradition in the Ancient Church." In *Bible, Church, Tradition: An Eastern Orthodox View*, 73–92. Belmont, MA: Nordland Publishing Co., 1972.

Izzo, Januarius M. *The Antimension in the Liturgical and Canonical Tradition of the Byzantine and Latin Churches*. Thesis ad Lauream n. 81. Rome: Pontificium Athenaeum Antonianum, 1975.

Karmiris, J. *The Status and Ministry of the Laity in the Orthodox Church*. Translated by E. Zachariades-Holmberg. Brookline, MA: Holy Cross Orthodox Press, 1994.

Klentos, J. "Rebaptizing Converts into the Orthodox Church: Old Perspectives on a New Problem." *Studia Liturgica* 29, no. 1 (1999): 216–34.

Κοτσώνης, Ἰ. [Cotsonis, Jerome]. Σημειώσεις κανονικοῦ δικαίου τῆς Ὀρθοδόξου Ἀνατολικῆς Ἐκκλησίας [*Canon Law Notes of the Eastern Orthodox Church*]. 3 vols. Thessaloniki: n.p., 1960–1962.

Kourides, Peter T. *The Evolution of the Greek Orthodox Church in America and Its Present Problems*. New York: Cosmos Greek-American Printing Company, 1959.

Meyendorff, J. "Contemporary Problems of Orthodox Canon Law." In *Living Tradition: Orthodox Witness in the Contemporary World*, 99–114. Crestwood, NY: St. Vladimir's Seminary Press, 1978.

Μίλας [Milaš], N. *Τὸ ἐκκλησιαστικὸν δίκαιον τῆς Ὀρθοδόξου Ἀνατολικῆς Ἐκκλησίας* [*The Ecclesiastical Law of the Eastern Orthodox Church*]. Translated by M. Ἀποστολόπουλος. Athens: Τύποις Π. Δ. Σακελλαρίου, 1906.

Μουρατίδης [Mouratides], Κ. *Κανονικὸν δίκαιον* [*Canon Law*]. Athens, 1960.

Papaioannou, G. "The Historical Development of the Greek Orthodox Archdiocese of North and South America." In *A Companion to the Greek Orthodox Church*, edited by F. Litsas, 178–206. New York: Greek Orthodox Archdiocese of North and South America, 1984.

Patelos, Constantin G., ed. *The Orthodox Church in the Ecumenical Movement*. Geneva: World Council of Churches, 1978.

Percival, H., ed. *The Seven Ecumenical Councils*. Vol. 14 of *Nicene and Post-Nicene Fathers*, second series. Grand Rapids, MI: Eerdmans, 1956.

Bishop Peter (L'Huillier). "The Reception of Roman Catholics into Orthodoxy." *St. Vladimir's Seminary Quarterly* 24 (1980): 75–82.

"The Proposed Charter: Progress and Potential." *Orthodox Observer* 67, no. 1189 (May 2002): 1, 3.

*Report to His Eminence Archbishop Iakovos Concerning the Future Theological Agenda of the Greek Orthodox Archdiocese*. Brookline, MA: Holy Cross Orthodox Press, 1990.

Ῥάλλης [Rhallēs], Γ.Α., and Μ. Ποτλῆς [Potlēs]. Σύνταγμα θείων καὶ ἱερῶν κανόνων τῶν τε ἁγίων καὶ πανευφήμων ἀποστόλων καὶ τῶν ἱερῶν οἰκουμενικῶν καὶ τοπικῶν συνόδων καὶ τῶν κατὰ μέρος ἁγίων πατέρων [*Collection of the Divine and Holy Canons of Both the Holy and Wholly Blessed Apostles, the Sacred Ecumenical and Local Synods and the Individual Holy Fathers*]. 6 vols. Athens: Γ. Χαρτοφύλαξ, 1852–1859.

Roeber, Anthony. *Mixed Marriages: An Orthodox History*. Yonkers, NY: Saint Vladimir's Seminary Press, 2018.

Rodopoulos, P. *An Overview of Orthodox Canon Law*. Rollinsford, NH: Orthodox Research Institute, 2007.

Stephanopoulos, R. *Guidelines for Orthodox Christians in Ecumenical Relations*. New York: SCOBA, 1973.

Θεοτοκᾶς, Μιχαὴλ [Theotokas, Michaēl]. Νομολογία τοῦ Οἰκουμενικοῦ Πατριαρχείου. Constantinople: Νεολόγου, 1897.

Treggiari, Susan. *Roman Marriage: Iusti Coniuges from the Time of Cicero to the Time of Ulpian*. Oxford: Clarendon, 1991.

Τρεμπέλας, Παναγιώτης [Trempelas, Panagiotis]. Μικρὸν εὐχολόγιον [*Small Euchologion*]. 2 vols. Athens: n.p., 1950, 1955.

Viscuso, Patrick, ed. and trans. *Guide for a Church under Islām: The Sixty-Six Canonical Questions Attributed to Theodōros Balsamōn*. Brookline, MA: Holy Cross Orthodox Press, 2014.

———. *Orthodox Canon Law: A Casebook for Study*. 2nd ed. Brookline, MA: Holy Cross Orthodox Press, 2011.

———. *Sexuality, Marriage, and Celibacy in Byzantine Law: The Alphabetical Collection of Matthew Blastarēs*. Brookline, MA: Holy Cross Orthodox Press, 2008.

Westerink, L. G., ed. and trans. *Nicholas I Patriarch of Constantinople: Miscellaneous Writings*. Washington, DC: Dumbarton Oaks, 1981.

Ζούστης, Βασίλειος Θ. [Zoustis, Basil T.]. *Ὁ ἐν Ἀμερικῇ Ἑλληνισμὸς καὶ ἡ δρᾶσις αὐτοῦ, Ἡ Ἱστορία τῆς Ἑλληνικῆς Ἀρχιεπισκοπῆς Ἀμερικῆς Βορείου καὶ Νοτίου* [*Hellenism in America and its Activity: The History of the Greek Archdiocese of North and South America*]. New York: D. C. Divry, Inc., 1954.

## INDEX OF NAMES

## Chalcedon

| | |
|---|---|
| 4 | 78n129 |
| 6 | 56 |
| 14 | 95n166 |
| 19 | 46, 47n56 |
| 26 | 90 |
| 27 | 103n179 |
| 28 | 32 |
| 29 | 67 |

## Code of Justinian

| | |
|---|---|
| 9.32.4 | 98n175 |

## 1 Constantinople (381) (Second Ecumenical Council)

| | |
|---|---|
| 7 | 96 |

## 2 Constantinople (553) (Fifth Ecumenical Council)

| | |
|---|---|
| 3 | 32 |

## 3 Constantinople (680) (Sixth Ecumenical Council)

| | |
|---|---|
| 2 | 33 |
| 95 | 138 |

## Constantinople (861) (Prōtodeutera)

| | |
|---|---|
| 7 | 46 |

## Constantinople (879)

| | |
|---|---|
| 3 | 60 |

## Digest

| | |
|---|---|
| 1.8.1 | 89n149 |
| 1.8.6 | 89n149 |
| 23.2 | 98n175 |

## Ephesus

| | |
|---|---|
| 8 | 32 |

## Gangra

| | |
|---|---|
| 21 | 29n24 |

## Gregory of Nyssa

| | |
|---|---|
| 4 | 49n61 |
| 5 | 49n61 |
| 8 | 49n61 |

## Holy Apostles (Apostolic Canons)

| | |
|---|---|
| 5 | 46, 47n56 |
| 14 | 66 |
| 17 | 58 |
| 18 | 58 |
| 19 | 58 |
| 29 | 57 |
| 30 | 57 |
| 37 | 46, 47n56 |
| 38 | 73, 90 |
| 41 | 73 |
| 42 | 60 |
| 44 | 28n22 |
| 47 | 92 |
| 50 | 92n154 |
| 79 | 58 |
| 80 | 57 |
| 81 | 61 |
| 84 | 47n55 |

## INDEX OF SUBJECTS

Printed in the USA
CPSIA information can be obtained
at www.ICGtesting.com
LVHW072117301023
762551LV00027B/1664